Answer Key & Commentary to

Introduction to

Classical &
New Testament Greek

Answer Key & Commentary to

Introduction to
Classical &
New Testament Greek

A Unified Approach

MICHAEL BOLER

THE CATHOLIC EDUCATION PRESS
Washington, D.C.

The paper used in this publication meets the requirements of American National
Standards for Information Science—Permanence of Paper for Printed Library Materials,
ANSI Z39.48-1992.

∞

ISBN: 978-1-949822-46-5
eISBN: 978-1-949822-47-2

Contents ∼

Introduction ∼

Introduction to Classical & New Testament Greek: A Unified Approach was initially published without an answer key. In the months after its publication, I began to receive inquiries about whether there existed an answer key. I was initially hesitant because I didn't want students to give up when they encountered difficult sentences and simply look up the answer in the answer key. Ideally, the instructor in the classroom should be there to provide guidance to students when they are stumped by a sentence. After some time and subsequent requests, I realized that my initial reluctance to provide an answer key was unwarranted. First, most of the requests that I received were from people who had bought the book to learn on their own and did not have access to a professor to walk them through the text. Second, even for a veteran teacher, learning to teach out of a textbook for the first time can take a considerable amount of preparation time. Finally, I became convinced that an answer key need not be a simple reference guide, but that it could in a small way replicate what I do in the classroom with my students.

Don't say "*the* translation."

Early in the semester, my students quickly learn never to ask me to repeat "the translation," but rather "a translation." While it may seem like I'm being pedantic, I firmly believe that the sooner a student realizes there is not one translation, the better. Because there is not a 1:1 correspondence between languages, in class we always discuss several different options for translating a given sentence. I have sought to replicate this experience in the writing of this companion volume. For many of the sentences you will see not one, but two or three translations, along with explanatory notes.

Methodology for Sentence Translations

Each chapter of *Introduction to Classical and New Testament Greek: A Unified Approach* contains 10 sentences, roughly half of which are taken from classical sources and the other half from the New Testament. For each sentence I try to give multiple translations, with the first being the most literal. Different instructors will have different preferences on how literally they want sentences to be translated. I tend to prefer that students try to be literal unless it sounds terrible. First and foremost, the sentence must make sense. Simply translating each word in order is not a literal translation. Let us look at the following example from chapter 3.

> μέγιστον ὀργῆς ἐστι φάρμακον ὁ λόγος. (Menander, Fragments)
> The word is the greatest remedy of anger.
> Reason is the greatest remedy of anger.
> Reason is the greatest remedy for anger.

It would clearly be terrible to translate this sentence "the greatest of anger is remedy reason," but any of the three translations are possible, especially when the sentence is a fragment without context. This is by no means an exhaustive list of possible translations. I also combine translation differences into one sentence. For example, since either "of" or "for" can be used to translate the genitive ὀργῆς in this sentence, I did not feel the need to add a 4th translation "The word is the greatest remedy for anger," since there is already an example where ὀργῆς is translated as "for anger."

Not Really a Translation

While we use the word "translation" to describe what we are doing with these sentences, we are in fact not really translating. Translation as we normally use the word means taking something written in one language and turning it into another language for an audience who does not know, nor is likely to learn, the original language. In such instances the translator needs to faithfully reproduce the meaning in another language, but he is immediately confronted with the question of how literally to translate. For example, since English generally prefers active to passive verbs, should a translator switch passive verbs to active verbs in a translation, or should he leave the passive nature of the original intact? If a word is used in a metaphor, should the translator translate the basic meaning of the word, or use the English equivalent of the metaphor? The aim of *Introduction to Classical and New Testament Greek: A Unified Approach* is to enable the student to read and understand Greek. Finer points of translation and translation theory are irrelevant if one does not first understand the Greek text. Ideally, as the student progresses in this book, he should become at times frustrated that the English does not as eloquently express the meaning of the sentence as the Greek original. Eventually, I give students permission to leave untranslated certain Greek words, such as λόγος, once they have a grasp of the range of meanings. Once again, the goal is to understand the Greek, not to produce the most literary translation in English.

Supplementary Exercises

The answers for the supplementary exercises are straightforward, with the exception of the English to Greek sentences at the end of every exercise. The sentences will all use vocabulary from their respective chapters, but the student is of course welcome to substitute any synonyms. Once again, the English to Greek sentences are possible translations, but are by no means the only translations.

Pronunciation Practice

At the start of each semester, I give my students the option of employing either the traditional pronunciation used in this book, or the modern Greek pronunciation. The topic of pronunciation is a controversial topic. The pronunciation used in this book is called "classical" by its proponents

and "Erasmian" by its detractors. The "modern" pronunciation will sometimes be called "Byzantine." I think a bit of humility is in order for all sides.
Obviously, pronunciation changes over thousands of years, but the "classical" pronunciation is at best an educated guess based on linguistic
evidence. There was a considerable difference between the pronunciation
of different dialects even in the classical era. These pronunciation differences were even more dramatic when Greek went from the language of
small geographical enclaves to the language of a massive empire under
Alexander the great and later the Eastern Roman empire. This massive
expansion of Greek is one of the reasons why finding a "Koine" or "bib-
lical" pronunciation is so difficult, as there were pronunciation differences
between the Greek spoken in Egypt, for example, and other regions. My
advice would be for any student primarily interested in Scripture, the
Church Fathers, or the Orthodox liturgy to use the Byzantine or modern
pronunciation. There are many websites on the internet where one can
learn this pronunciation. For those who are studying Greek primarily to
read classical sources, I would suggest using the one in this book. You can
also find recordings of vocabulary and selected texts using the classical
pronunciation on many internet sites. Most of my students have found
the one used in this book to be the easiest.

A Final Note

As you work your way through *Introduction to Classical and New
Testament Greek: A Unified Approach*, try to resist the urge to immediately consult this companion volume at the first sign of difficulty. Part
of learning to read Greek is struggling to make sense of the sentence. If
you turn to the answer at the first sign of trouble, you will lose the valuable
experience of thinking your way through the sentence. Even the frustra-
tion is valuable. There is of course a limit to all things, so if you are completely stumped, or if you wish to check your answer, then consult this
volume.

Chapter 2 ~

Sentences

1. ὁ θεὸς ἀγάπη ἐστίν. (1 John 4:8)
God is love.
- While there are some exceptions, the general rule is that when you have a subject and a predicate nominative, an X is Y statement, the subject gets the definite article, so "God is love." Often you can't translate the definite article in your English translation.

2. ὁ φόβος ἐστὶ προσδοκία κακοῦ. (Chrysippus, *Fragments*)
Fear is the expectation of evil.
- Another example where it is not possible to translate the definite article. Greek prefers to use the definite article where English does not. One example is the definite article with abstract nouns, as in this sentence with "fear."
- As will become clear in the following chapters, cases like the genitive and dative often require the use of a preposition in your English translation. As with the case of all the notes, use the given translation in the notes as a place-holder until you learn the grammatical concept.

3. φόβος οὐκ ἔστιν ἐν τῇ ἀγάπῃ. (1 John 4:18)
Fear does not exist in love.
There is no fear in love.

- The first translation is preferable, because it does not change the grammatical construction of the sentence.
- Most of the time when you see some form of the word εἰμί, you will have a subject and a predicative nominative, as in the first two sentences. Occasionally, however, you will see a form of εἰμί used in the sense of "exists," as in this example. You can still translate it as "is," but often "exists" is preferable.

4. ἐγώ εἰμι ἡ ὁδὸς καὶ ἡ ἀλήθεια καὶ ἡ ζωή. (John 14:6)
I am the way and the truth and the life.
I am the way, the truth, and the life.

- When the context makes clear the subject and the predicate nominative, you will often see the definite article used in the predicate, seemingly violating the rule established in the first two examples. This is most common with 1st and 2nd person subjects. The context will always make the subject obvious.

5. ἐγὼ καὶ ὁ πατὴρ ἕν ἐσμεν. (John 10:30)
I and the Father are one.
The Father and I, we are one.

- Most of the time, when you see a plural verb, you will have a plural subject. Sometimes you will see two singular subjects take a plural verb. The same occurs in English. We say "Jack and Jill ran up the hill," and not "Jack and Jill runs up the hill."

6. σὺ εἶ ὁ υἱὸς τοῦ θεοῦ. (John 1:49)
You are the son of God.
See the note on sentence 4 above.

7. ἡ εὐδαιμονία ἐστὶν εὔροια βίου. (Zeno of Citium, in Stobaeus, *Anthology*)
Happiness is the good flow of life.
Happiness is the prosperous flow of life.
Happiness is the free flow of life.

- Here the rule applies where the subject gets the definite article and the predicate nominative does not. In your translation, however, the English is reversed. While this seems confusing at first, it will become easier as you become more familiar with the grammatical concepts. This is precisely why it is so important to understand what you are reading, then to translate it. Let your understanding of the grammar lead your translation; don't let your translation lead your understanding of the grammar.

8. λύπης ἰατρός ἐστιν ὁ φίλος. (Menander, *Fragments*)
The friend is a physician of grief.
A friend is the physician of grief.

- We know that the friend is the subject of the sentence, and the physician is the predicate nominative. We know this because of which noun takes the definite article. In an inflectional language like Greek, it doesn't matter which word comes first.

9. ὁ ὕπνος ἐστὶ σωμάτων σωτηρία. (Menander, *Fragments*)
Sleep is the preservation of bodies.
Sleep is the salvation of bodies.
Sleep is the preservation of the body.

- I'm generally not a fan of using collective singular nouns to translate Greek plural nouns, as in the third translation here. It is better at the beginning of your Greek journey to keep singular nouns singular and plural nouns plural. As long as you understand the grammar, however, it can occasionally be OK.

10. ἡ προπέτεια πολλοῖς ἐστιν αἰτία κακῶν. (Menander, *Fragments*)
Rashness is a cause of evils for many.
Rashness is a cause of evils for many people.
Haste is the cause of evils for many.
Rashness is for many a cause of evils.

- Once again, you are not bound to replicate the precise word order in your translations.

- Just as in English, the implied noun "people" is often left unspoken, e.g. "Coffee is necessary for many." We know that this example means many people, not many dogs, or many cars, etc.

Supplementary Exercises

Change the following verbs into the plural.

    a. ἐσμέν   b. εἰσί(ν)   c. ἐστέ

Change the following verbs into the singular.

    a. εἶ   b. ἐστίν   c. εἰμί

Write the corresponding definite article next to the following nouns.

ἡ ἀγάπη	ὁ λόγος
ἡ ἀλήθεια	ὁ νόμος
ἡ ἀρετή	ἡ σοφία
τὸ βιβλίον	ἡ χαρά
τὸ ἔργον	ἡ ψυχή

Translate the following sentences into Greek.

In the examples below, multiple versions are given to show that one is not bound by word order in Greek, although the preference is subject, verb, then predicate.

1. Wisdom is joy.

ἡ σοφία χαρά ἐστιν.

ἡ σοφία ἐστὶ χαρά.

χαρά ἐστι ἡ σοφία.

2. The Spirit is life.

ἡ ψυχὴ ζωή ἐστιν.

ἡ ψυχή ἐστι ζωή.

3. Excellence and truth exist.

ἡ ἀρετὴ καὶ ἡ ἀλήθειά εἰσιν.

4. A book is a gift.
βιβλίον ἐστὶ δῶρον.

5. The law is a gift.
ὁ νόμος δῶρόν ἐστιν.
ὁ νόμος ἐστὶ δῶρον.

Chapter 3 ~

Sentences

1. ἐγώ εἰμι ὁ ἄρτος τῆς ζωῆς. (John 6:35)
I am the bread of life.

2. αἱ ἡδοναί εἰσι φθαρταί, αἱ τιμαί εἰσιν ἀθάνατοι. (Periander, in Diogenes Laertius, *Lives of Eminent Philosophers*)
Pleasures are perishable; honors are immortal.

3. ἐγὼ οὐκ εἰμὶ ὁ Χριστός. (John 1:20)
I am not the Christ.
I am not the Messiah.

4. ἀθάνατος ἡ ψυχή ἐστιν. (Clement of Rome, *First Homily*)
The soul is immortal.
Immortal is the soul.

5. τὸ μέτρον ἐστὶν ἄριστον. (Cleobulus, in Diogenes Laertius, *Lives of Eminent Philosophers*)
The mean is the best.
Moderation is best.

6. ὁ χρόνος ἰατρὸς τῶν πόνων ἐστίν. (Menander, *Fragments*)
Time is the physician of sufferings.
Time is the healer of grief.

- For the second translation, see chapter 2, sentence 9 for the use of singular collective nouns.

7. τῷ σοφῷ ξένον οὐδέν ἐστιν. (Antisthenes, in Diogenes Laertius, *Lives of Eminent Philosophers*)
Nothing is strange to the wise man.
For the wise man, nothing is foreign.

8. θεοῦ γάρ ἐσμεν συνεργοί. (1 Cor. 3:9)
For we are co-workers of God.
For we are God's helpers.

9. ἀνελεύθεροι γάρ εἰσιν οἱ φιλάργυροι. (Menander, *Fragments*)
For the greedy are not free.
For the greedy are unfree.

10. μέγιστον ὀργῆς ἐστι φάρμακον ὁ λόγος. (Menander, *Fragments*)
The word is the greatest remedy of anger.
Reason is the greatest remedy of anger.
Reason is the greatest remedy for anger.

Supplementary Exercises

To which case do the following short descriptions apply?

"of" case	Genitive	"to/for" case	Dative
"object" case	Accusative	"address" case	Vocative
"subject" case	Nominative		

Give the case and number for each of the following noun forms. Some forms have more than one answer.

ψυχῆς	Genitive	Singular	λόγος	Nominative	Singular
ψυχῶν	Genitive	Plural	λόγε	Vocative	Singular
ψυχάς	Accusative	Plural	λόγοι	Nominative	Plural
ψυχαί	Nominative	Plural	λόγων	Genitive	Plural
ψυχῇ	Dative	Singular	λόγον	Accusative	Singular
χαρᾷ	Dative	Singular	βιβλίον	Nominative	Singular
χαρά	Nominative	Singular		Accusative	Singular
χαραῖς	Dative	Plural	βιβλίου	Genitive	Singular
χαράς	Accusative	Plural	βιβλία	Nominative	Plural
χαράν	Accusative	Singular		Accusative	Plural

In the chart above, blank spaces are alternate answers of the entry immediately above, e.g. βιβλίον is both the nominative singular and accusative singular form. While not reflected in the chart, the vocative is identical to the nominative in all the above nouns except λόγος.

For each of the following nouns, give the corresponding forms of the definite article and the adjective καλός.

ὁ	καλὸς	λόγος	τὰ	καλὰ	βιβλία
τὸν	καλὸν	λόγον	τῇ	καλῇ	ψυχῇ
τοὺς	καλοὺς	λόγους	τῆς	καλῆς	ψυχῆς
τὸ	καλὸν	βιβλίον	ταῖς	καλαῖς	χαραῖς
τῶν	καλῶν	βιβλίων	τὴν	καλὴν	χαράν

Translate the following sentences into Greek.

1. Honor is immortal.

ἡ τιμή ἐστιν ἀθάνατος.

- Remember that adjectives like ἀθάνατος, –ον do not have separate feminine endings, so ἡ τιμή ἐστιν ἀθανάτη would be incorrect.

2. Life is strange.

ὁ βίος ἐστὶ ξένος.

3. The pleasure of anger is evil.

ἡ ἡδονὴ τῆς ὀργῆς ἐστι κακή.
κακή ἐστιν ἡ ἡδονὴ τῆς ὀργῆς.
κακὴ ἡ ἡδονὴ τῆς ὀργῆς ἐστιν.

4. Anger is bad for the good life.

ἡ ὀργή ἐστι κακὴ τῷ ἀγάθῳ βίῳ.
τῷ ἀγάθῳ βίῳ ἡ ὀργή ἐστι κακή.
τῷ ἀγάθῳ βίῳ ἡ ὀργὴ κακή ἐστιν.

5. Base pleasure is not immortal.

ἡ κακὴ ὀργὴ οὐκ ἔστιν ἀθάνατος.
οὐκ ἀθάνατός ἐστιν ἡ κακὴ ὀργή.

Chapter 4 ∼

Sentences

1. κακὸν φέρουσι καρπὸν οἱ κακοὶ φίλοι. (Menander, *Fragments*)
Bad friends bear bad fruit.
Evil friends bring forth evil fruit.

2. ἀργὸς μὴ ἴσθι. (Thales, in Stobaeus, *Anthology*)
Don't be lazy.
Be not lazy.

3. ὁ δὲ θεὸς γινώσκει τὰς καρδίας ὑμῶν. (Luke 16:15)
But God knows your hearts.

4. ὁ ἀναμάρτητος ὑμῶν πρῶτος ἐπ' αὐτὴν βαλέτω λίθον. (John 8:7)
Let the sinless one of you first throw the stone at her.
The sinless among you, let him first throw the stone at her.
   • Notice that the adjective "first" modifies the "sinless one", not "stone." If it were "first stone," it would be πρῶτον, not πρῶτος.

5. λέγει αὐτῷ Σίμων Πέτρος, "Κύριε, ποῦ ὑπάγεις;" (John 13:36)
Simon Peter says to him, "Lord, where are you going?"
Simon Peter says to him, "Lord, where do you go?"
   • As you will see in the chapter on aspect (chapter 12), the present tense is usually translated as a simple present, e.g. "reads, sings" etc. Occasionally you will encounter a present tense with imperfect

aspect and the context will require you to translate it as "are reading, are singing," etc. As a general rule, try translating the present tense the simple way (aorist aspect) unless you feel the context dictates the "are . . .ing" translation. Right now, don't be confused by the terms aorist and imperfect.

6. μεγαλύνει ἡ ψυχή μου τὸν κύριον. (Luke 1:46)
My soul magnifies the Lord.

7. σὺ εἶ ὁ υἱός μου ὁ ἀγαπητός. (Luke 3:22)
You are my beloved son.
You are my son, my beloved son.

8. εἰ υἱὸς εἶ τοῦ θεοῦ, βάλε σεαυτὸν κάτω. (Matthew 4:6)
If you are the son of God, throw yourself downwards.
If you are the son of God, cast yourself down.

9. δίωκε δόξην καὶ ἀρετήν, φεῦγε δὲ ψόγον. (Menander, *Fragments*)
Pursue glory and excellence, flee censure.
Pursue glory and excellence, but flee blame.

10. ἔστω δὲ ὁ λόγος ὑμῶν ναὶ ναί, οὒ οὔ. (Matthew 5:37)
But let your word yes be yes and your word no be no.
But let your yes mean yes and your no mean no.

Supplementary Exercises

Give the person, number, and mood for the following forms of λύω.

λύω	1st Person	Singular	Indicative
λύομεν	1st Person	Plural	Indicative
λυόντων	3rd Person	Plural	Imperative
λύει	3rd Person	Singular	Indicative
λῦε	2nd Person	Singular	Imperative

λύουσι	3rd Person	Plural	Indicative
λύεις	2nd Person	Singular	Indicative
λυέτω	3rd Person	Singular	Imperative
λύετε	2nd Person	Plural	Indicative
	2nd Person	Plural	Imperative

Give the corresponding 2nd person personal pronoun for the following 1st person personal pronouns.

1st Person	2nd Person	1st Person	2nd Person
ἐγώ	σύ	ἡμᾶς	ὑμᾶς
ἐμέ	σέ	ἐμοῦ	σοῦ
ἡμεῖς	ὑμεῖς		

Give the corresponding 1st person personal pronoun for the following 2nd person personal pronouns.

2nd Person	1st Person	2nd Person	1st Person
σοῦ	ἐμοῦ	σέ	ἐμέ
ὑμῖν	ἡμῖν	σοί	ἐμοί
ὑμῶν	ἡμῶν		

Translate the following sentences into Greek.

1. The Lord knows the heart of people.
ὁ κύριος γιγνώσκει τὴν καρδίαν τῶν ἀνθρώπων.

2. Don't (plural) throw stones.
μὴ βάλλετε λίθους.

3. The blameless son knows the beloved father.
ὁ ἀναμάρτητος υἱὸς γιγνώσκει τὸν ἀγαπητὸν πατέρα.
ὁ υἱὸς ὁ ἀναμάρτητος γιγνώσκει τὸν ἀγαπητὸν πατέρα.

- πατέρα is the accusative singular of a 3rd declension noun, introduced in chapter 8. It was accidentally included in this exercise, yet it illustrates an important point concerning the importance of the definite article. If you saw this sentence and did not recognize the 3rd declension noun, the presence of the definite article τόν tells you that πατέρα must be a masculine singular accusative noun.

- The first example uses the more common definite article + adjective + noun construction. The second example uses the definite article + noun + definite article + adjective construction. They are translated the same in English. Attributive position only means the adjective is preceded by the definite article. Both examples have the adjective in the attributive position. τὸν ἀγαπητὸν πατέρα could have also been expressed with τὸν πατέρα τὸν ἀγαπητόν.

4. A stone does not bring forth fruit.

ὁ λίθος οὐ φέρει τοὺς καρπούς.

λίθος οὐ φέρει καρπούς.

οὐ φέρει τοὺς καρποὺς ὁ λίθος.

- The Greek indefinite pronoun τις (chapter 25) doesn't really correspond to the English "a/an." Greek also uses the definite article where English does not. In the beginning it is helpful to express something like "a stone" with the noun without the definite article. It is also perfectly fine to use the article if you prefer. Likewise, in sentences such as this, English objects without the English definite article, e.g. "fruit," can be expressed with or without the definite article in Greek.

5. If you know the Lord, you know human beings.

εἰ γιγνώσκεις τὸν κύριον, γιγνώσκεις τοὺς ἀνθρώπους.

6. We know, but we do not speak.

γιγνώσκομεν, δὲ οὐ λέγομεν.

Chapter 5 ~

Sentences

1. ἡ βασιλεία τοῦ θεοῦ ἐντὸς ὑμῶν ἐστιν. (Luke 17:21)
The kingdom of God is within you.

2. τῆς λύπης ἰατρός ἐστιν ἀνθρώποις ὁ λόγος. (Menander, *Fragments*)
Reason is the physician of grief for men.
The word is the physician of grief for men.
For humans, reason is the physician of grief.
- ἄνθρωπος can be translated as "man" if you understand that it is not exclusively referring to males. Men, humans, people, are all perfectly fine translations of ἄνθρωπος in the plural.

3. ἡ παιδεία ἐν ταῖς εὐτυχίαις ἐστὶ κόσμος, ἐν δὲ ταῖς ἀτυχίαις καταφυγή.
(Aristotle, in Diogenes Laertius, *Lives of Eminent Philosophers*)
Education is an ornament in successes, and an escape in misfortunes.
Education is an ornament in success, and an escape in misfortune.
- Sometimes for the sake of not having an awkward translation, it is permissible to translate Greek plurals as a collective singular. Especially for beginning students, I recommend translating as literally as possible unless it sounds awkward. Remember that we are using translation as the means to the end of understanding Greek. Taking liberties with the translation is fine if you understand why you are taking liberties. What must be avoided is not paying attention to

the difference between singular and plural and committing the cardinal sin of language study, getting the "gist of it" and not paying attention to detail.

4. τυφλὴ καὶ δύστηνος ἀνθρώποις ἡ τύχη ἐστίν. (Menander, *Fragments*)
Fortune is blind and disastrous for men.
Blind and disastrous for men is fortune.

- Remember that when you translate τύχη as "fortune," it doesn't mean "riches," but rather something akin to "chance."
- As you read in the appendix "How to read a Greek sentence," it is always important to pay attention to the Greek word order to appreciate the overall artistry of the sentence. In the beginning you want to avoid strict word order translation. The most important thing is to understand the meaning of the sentence, and this is best done by translating with natural English word order. That does not mean, however, that you should not appreciate the effect that the order of the Greek sentence would have upon the reader or audience. This is a line of a play, and so the audience would hear that something was blind and disastrous for human beings, but what exactly is blind and disastrous is delayed until the end of the line.

5. δὸς δόξαν τῷ θεῷ. (John 9:24)
Give glory to God.

- As we can see, the New Testament includes the definite article when it refers to God. It is not necessary to translate it every time as "the God."

6. ἄγει πρὸς τὸ φῶς τὴν ἀλήθειαν ὁ χρόνος. (Menander, *Fragments*)
Time leads the truth towards the light.
Time leads truth towards the light.

- Notice here that the subject of the sentence, time, is the last word of the line. The audience would have to wait until the end to grasp the full meaning of the sentence. Again, natural English word order is preferable to "Leads towards the light the truth does time." This translation is not incorrect, but I find that a strict adherence to word order in translation is often an impediment to a beginning student's grasp of the language.

7. κύριός ἐστιν τοῦ σαββάτου ὁ υἱὸς τοῦ ἀνθρώπου. (Luke 6:5)
The son of man is lord of the Sabbath.

8. μακάριοι οἱ καθαροὶ τῇ καρδίᾳ. (Matthew 5:8)
Happy are the pure in heart.
Blessed are the pure in heart.
Fortunate are the pure in heart.
Blessed are the pure of heart.

9. ἔργοις φιλόπονος ἴσθι, μὴ λόγοις μόνον. (Menander, *Fragments*)
In works be fond of toil, not only in words.
Be fond of work in deeds and not only in words.

10. δίκαιος ἴσθι καὶ τοῖς φίλοις καὶ τοῖς ξένοις. (Menander, *Fragments*)
Be just to both friends and strangers.
Be just to friends and strangers.

- It sounds odd to English ears, but where we prefer expressions like "both ... and," and "neither ... nor," Greek prefers the more natural "and ... and," and "neither ... neither." Of course it would sound awkward to translate that literally, so it is permissible to alter the construction a bit.

Supplementary Exercises

Would you use a dative of indirect object or a dative of respect to translate into Greek the following English sentences?

1. Writing is difficult for students.	*dative of respect*
2. Give glory to God.	*dative of indirect object*
3. Silence is difficult for teachers.	*dative of respect*
4. The doctor gave advice to the patient.	*dative of indirect object*
5. Patience is difficult for doctors.	*dative of respect*

Would you use a genitive of possession or an objective genitive to translate the following English phrases?

1. The love of glory	*objective genitive*
2. The glory of God	*genitive of possession*
3. The kingdom of heaven	*genitive of possession*
4. Hatred of grief	*objective genitive*

Translate the following sentences into Greek.

βάλλω = to throw | γιγνώσκω = to know | εἰμί = to be | λέγω = to speak

1. Glory in grief speaks to the world.

ἡ δόξα ἐν λύπῃ λέγει τῳ κόσμῳ.

2. Don't (singular) throw education to chance.

μὴ βάλλε τὴν παιδείαν τῃ τύχῃ.

3. The art of education knows moderation.

ἡ τέχνη τῆς παιδείας γιγνώσκει τὸ μέτρον.

4. Chance does not know moderation.

ἡ τύχη οὐ γιγνώσκει τὸ μέτρον.

οὐ γιγνώσκει τὸ μέτρον ἡ τύχη.

5. Glory after grief is blessed.

ἡ δόξα μετὰ λύπην ἐστὶ μακάρια.

μακάρια ἡ δόξα μετὰ λύπην.

- In many proverbs and aphorisms the word "is" is implied and not written.

6. Blessed are the doctors.

μακάριοί εἰσιν οἱ ἰατροί.

οἱ ἰατροί εἰσι μακάριοι.

μακάριοι οἱ ἰατροί.

Chapter 6 ～

Sentences

1. αὐτὸς γὰρ ὁ πατὴρ φιλεῖ ὑμᾶς. (John 16:27)
For the Father himself loves you.
   - Most of the time, "himself, herself, itself, themselves" works as a suitable translation for the intensive pronoun. Occasionally another construction "the very man, etc." is merited to capture the sense of the intensive.

2. κοινὰ τὰ τῶν φίλων ἐστίν. (Traditional Proverb)
Common are the things of friends.
The property of friends is in common.
   - This common use of the definite article τά and a genitive can be tricky to translate. "Things," is usually the most straightforward translation.

3. χαλεπὰ τὰ καλά ἐστιν. (Traditional Proverb)
Beautiful things are difficult.
Difficult are beautiful things.

4. μέτρον τοῦ βίου τὸ καλόν ἐστιν, οὐ τὸ τοῦ χρόνου μῆκος. (Plutarch, *Moralia*)
The beautiful is the measure of life, not length of time.
Beauty is the measure of life, not the length of time.
The measure of life is the beautiful, not the length of time.

5. ὁ ἀγαθὸς ἄνθρωπος ἐκ τοῦ ἀγαθοῦ θησαυροῦ τῆς καρδίας προφέρει τὸ ἀγαθόν, καὶ ὁ πονηρὸς ἐκ τοῦ πονηροῦ προφέρει τὸ πονηρόν. (Luke 6:45)

The good man brings forth good from the good treasury of his heart, and the wicked man brings forth wickedness from the wicked treasury of his heart.

The good man brings forth the good from the good treasury of his heart, and the wicked brings forth the wicked from the wicked (treasury of his heart).

- Translating neuter singular substantive adjectives can be tricky. Sometimes a literal translation is best "the good," but it is permissible to use a noun in its place, e.g. "goodness." If you chose to use a noun, just be sure to remember that it is a substantive adjective.

6. πάντα τῶν θεῶν ἐστι· φίλοι δὲ τοῖς σοφοῖς οἱ θεοί· κοινὰ δὲ τὰ τῶν φίλων· πάντα ἄρα τῶν σοφῶν. (Diogenes the Cynic, in Diogenes Laertius, *Lives of Eminent Philosophers*)

All things are of the gods. And the gods are friends to the wise. And common are the things of friends. Therefore, all things are of the wise.

All things belong to the gods. The gods are friends to the wise. Common are the things of friends. Therefore, all things belong to the wise.

- The genitive of possession here can be translated literally (1st translation) or more liberally (2nd translation).
- δὲ is a ubiquitous word in Greek that is sometimes hard to translate. Greek loves to have some word connecting a sentence to the previous sentence. In English this is frowned upon. For beginning students, I generally encourage students to translate all the words lest the bad habit of skipping troublesome little words becomes engrained. In cases such as this, however, I never penalize students for omitting them, as in the second translation.

7. φίλοις εὐτυχοῦσι καὶ ἀτυχοῦσιν ὁ αὐτὸς ἴσθι. (Periander, in Stobaeus, *Anthology*)

To friends fortunate and unfortunate, be the same.

Be the same to fortunate and unfortunate friends.

Be the same person to fortunate and unfortunate friends.

8. περὶ τῶν αὐτῶν οὐδέποτε τὰ αὐτὰ λέγεις. (Socrates, in Xenophon, *Memorabilia*)

You never say the same things about the same things.

- You could theoretically translate τῶν αὐτῶν as "same people," since the genitive plural is the same for all three genders. The context of the conversation, however, indicates that something like "topics" is meant for both neuter uses of αὐτῶν here. You would, of course, not be expected to know this.

9. ὁ Σωκράτης αὐτός ἐστιν καὶ ὁ ἄνθρωπος καὶ τὸ ζῷον. (Aristotle, *Metaphysics*)

Socrates himself is both a man and an animal.

Socrates himself is a human and an animal.

10. λέγει ἡ μήτηρ τοῦ Ἰησοῦ πρὸς αὐτόν, "Οἶνον οὐκ ἔχουσιν." (John 2:3)

The mother of Jesus says to him, "They have no wine."

- If the subject from a verb is obvious from the context, Greek will often omit it. As the notes indicate, the context of this sentence makes it clear the hosts are the subject of ἔχουσιν.

Supplementary Exercises

Give the case and number of the following nouns.

μαθητής	nominative	singular	θαλάττης	genitive	singular
νεανίου	genitive	singular	θάλαττα	nominative	singular
νεανιῶν	genitive	plural	μαθητοῦ	genitive	singular
νεανίαι	nominative	plural	μαθητάς	accusative	plural
θαλάττας	accusative	plural			

Identify the function of αὐτός in the following sentences. Is it (1) a personal pronoun, (2) an intensive adjective, or (3) an adjective meaning "the same"?

1. ὁ Ἰησοῦς αὐτὸς λέγει.   (2) intensive adjective
2. γιγνώσκομεν τὸν αὐτὸν φίλον. (3) an adjective meaning "the same"
3. τὰ ζῷα αὐτὰ οὐ λέγουσιν.   (2) intensive adjective
4. μὴ λεγέτω αὐτῷ ὁ μαθητής.   (1) personal pronoun
5. ὁ Ἰησοῦς λέγει αὐτοῖς.   (1) personal pronoun

Translate the following sentences into Greek.
βάλλω = to throw | γιγνώσκω = to know | εἰμί = to be |λέγω = to speak

1. Wine is a difficult friend.
ὁ οἰνός ἐστι χαλεπὸς φίλος.

2. The student has the same treasure.
ὁ μαθητὴς ἔχει τὸν αὐτὸν θησαυρόν.

3. The animals themselves speak.
τὰ ζῷα αὐτὰ λέγει.
  • Remember that neuter plural subjects take singular verbs.

4. Jesus speaks to her.
ὁ Ἰησοῦς λέγει αὐτῇ.
ὁ Ἰησοῦς λέγει πρὸς αὐτήν.

5. We have the same common treasure.
ἔχομεν τὸν αὐτὸν θησαυρόν.
τὸν αὐτὸν θησαυρὸν ἔχομεν.

6. Don't (singular) throw the wine at wicked friends.
μὴ βάλλε τὸν οἰνον τοῖς κακοῖς φίλοις.

7. I do not know an evil animal.
οὐ γιγνώσκω κακὸν ζῷον.

Chapter 7 ～

Sentences

1. ἄδικόν ἐστιν τὸ λυπεῖν τοὺς φίλους. (Menander, *Fragments*)
It is unjust to grieve friends.
   - Here grieve is used in the sense of causing grief, not feeling grief.
It is unjust to cause friends pain.

2. καλῶν οὐδὲν ἄνευ πόνου καὶ ἐπιμελείας οἱ θεοὶ νέμουσιν ἀνθρώποις. (Prodicus, *Fragments*)
The gods give nothing to humans without toil and diligence.
   - The toil and diligence meant here is the toil and diligence of humans.

3. ἐκεῖνον δεῖ αὐξάνειν, ἐμὲ δὲ ἐλαττοῦσθαι. (John 3:30)
That one must increase, but I must decrease.
It is necessary that he increase and I decrease.
It is necessary for that one to increase and for me to decrease.

4. τὸ πολλὰ πράττειν ἐστὶ πανταχοῦ σαπρόν. (Menander, *Fragments*)
To do many things is absolutely unsound.
Doing many things is absolutely unsound.
It is absolutely unsound to do many things.

5. δίκαιος εἶναι μᾶλλον ἢ χρηστὸς θέλε. (Menander, *Fragments*)
Wish to be just rather than useful.

6. οὐ θέλω διὰ μέλανος καὶ καλάμου σοι γράφειν. (3 John 1:13)
I do not wish to write to you through ink and pen.
I don't want to write to you with ink and pen.

7. αἱ δ᾽ ἐλπίδες βόσκουσι τοὺς κενοὺς βροτῶν. (Menander, *Fragments*)
But hopes feed the empty of men.
But hopes feed empty men.

8. ἄρτι μανθάνω. (Euripides, *Alcestis*)
Now I understand.

9. γὰρ τὸ ζῆν Χριστὸς καὶ τὸ ἀποθανεῖν κέρδος. (Phil. 1:21)
For to me to live is Christ and to die is gain.

10. ὁ δὲ διὰ τὸ μένειν αὐτὸν εἰς τὸν αἰῶνα ἀπαράβατον ἔχει τὴν ἱερωσύνην. (Heb 7:24)
But he, on account of him remaining into the age, holds an eternal priesthood.
But he, because he remains forever, has an eternal priesthood.

Supplementary Exercises

Indicate whether the infinitives in the following sentences are complementary infinitives or articular infinitives.

1. δεῖ τῷ διδασκάλῳ γράφειν.	complementary infinitive
2. ὁ πόνος τοῦ γράφειν χρηστός ἐστιν.	articular infinitive
3. τὸ τὰ ἄδικα πράττειν ἐστὶ κενὸν τοῖς βροτοῖς.	articular infinitive
4. οἱ διδάσκαλοι οὐκ ἐθέλουσιν μανθάνειν.	complementary infinitive
5. ἐθέλομεν πράττειν τὰ δίκαια.	complementary infinitive

Translate the following sentences into Greek.

1. Don't (plural) deal out injustice to the teacher.

μὴ νέμετε ἀδικίαν τῷ διδασκάλῳ.

μὴ νέμετε τὴν ἀδικίαν τῷ διδασκάλῳ.

2. It is useful to remain.

χρηστόν ἐστι τὸ μένειν.

3. Let the unjust men among us not increase.

μὴ αὐξανόντων οἱ ἄδικοι ἡμῶν.

4. It is necessary to learn just things.

δεῖ μανθάνειν τὰ δίκαια.

5. The men want to write empty things.

οἱ ἄνθρωποι ἐθέλουσι γράφειν τὰ κενά.

6. I don't understand.

οὐ μανθάνω.

Chapter 8 ～

Sentences

1. στέρησις δέ ἐστιν αἰσθήσεως ὁ θάνατος. (Epicurus, *Letter to Menoeceus*)
Death is the deprivation of sense-perception.
Death is the loss of sense perception.
   - Remember that the vocabulary entries in this book are simplified. If a synonym to a vocabulary entry seems to fit the sense of the Greek better, use it. Just be sure you are expressing what the Greek says and not what you wish it had said.

2. κατὰ τὴν ἰδίαν φρόνησιν οὐδεὶς εὐτυχεῖ. (Menander, *Fragments*)
No one is fortunate according to their own thought.
No one is lucky in their own opinion.

3. χάρις ὑμῖν καὶ εἰρήνη ἀπὸ θεοῦ πατρὸς ἡμῶν καὶ κυρίου Ἰησοῦ Χριστοῦ. (1 Cor 1:3)
Grace to you and peace from God our Father and the Lord Jesus Christ.
Grace and peace be to you from God our Father and the Lord Jesus Christ.

4. ἡ χάρις τοῦ κυρίου Ἰησοῦ μεθ' ὑμῶν. (1 Cor 16:23)
The grace of the Lord Jesus be with you.

5. ἀνάπαυσίς ἐστι τῶν κακῶν ἀπραξία. (Menander, *Fragments*)
Inaction is rest from evils.

6. ἡ πίστις χωρὶς τῶν ἔργων ἀργή ἐστιν. (James 2:20)
Faith without works is lazy.
Faith without works is idle.
Faith without works is useless.
  • This is not the famous "Faith without works is dead," which occurs later in James 2:26.

7. βουλὴ πονηρὰ χρηστὸν οὐκ ἔχει τέλος. (Menander, *Fragments*)
A wicked plan does not have a useful end.

8. τὰ σώματα ὑμῶν μέλη Χριστοῦ ἐστιν. (1 Cor 6:15)
Your bodies are limbs of Christ.
  • Aside from sounding silly, you know "Your limbs are the bodies of Christ" is incorrect because σώματα, not μέλη, has the definite article τὰ.

9. ξίφος τιτρώσκει σῶμα, τὸν δὲ νοῦν λόγος. (Menander, *Fragments*)
A sword wounds the body, but a word wounds the mind.
A sword wounds the body, but *logos* wounds the mind.
  • At a certain point, I give my students permission to just say *logos* rather than picking an English translation. Remember, this is the ultimate goal in your journey in Greek: the ability to have in your mind the original word with all its meanings. Using translations is just a means to get you to that goal.

10. βλέπομεν γὰρ ἄρτι δι᾽ ἐσόπτρου ἐν αἰνίγματι, τότε δὲ πρόσωπον πρὸς πρόσωπον. (1 Cor 13:12)
For now we see in an enigma through a mirror, but then face to face.
  • This very literal translation is obviously clunky. Two things make a literal translation of this line difficult. The first is the adverbial use of the prepositional phrase ἐν αἰνίγματι. The second is the technological difference between a mirror in the ancient world and a modern-day mirror. While mirrors today are quite good, ancient mirrors, depending on the quality, could be quite dark and give poor and warped reflections.

For now we see enigmatically through a mirror, but then we shall see face to face.

Supplemental Exercises

To what declension do the following nouns belong?

τέλος	3rd Declension	σῶμα	3rd Declension
θάνατος	2nd Declension	χαρά	1st Declension
γένος	3rd Declension	δαίμων	3rd Declension
μαθητής	1st Declension	ἐλπίς	3rd Declension
Σωκράτης	3rd Declension		

Change the following singular nouns to the plural.

δαίμονος	δαιμόνων	γένει	γενῶν
σῶμα	σώματα	βασιλεύς	βασιλεῖς
πόλεως	πόλεων		

Change the following plural nouns to the singular.

δαίμονες	δαίμων	γένη	γένος
σώματα	σῶμα	βασιλέας	βασιλέα
πόλεων	πόλεως		

Translate the following sentences into Greek.

1. The death of Socrates teaches generations.
    ὁ θάνατος τοῦ Σωκράτους παιδεύει τοὺς αἰῶνας.

2. Do you (singular) see the hope of the city?
    βλέπεις τὴν ἐλπίδα τῆς πόλεως;

3. Faith teaches wisdom.

ἡ πίστις παιδεύει σοφίαν.

ἡ πίστις παιδεύει τὴν σοφίαν.

4. The divinities see the deaths of kings.

οἱ δαίμονες βλέπουσι τοὺς θανάτους τῶν βασιλέων.

5. Grace is not private.

ἡ χαρὰ οὐκ ἔστιν ἴδια.

6. Mothers teach fathers.

αἱ μητέρες παιδεύουσι τοὺς πατέρας.

αἱ μητέρες πατέρας παιδεύουσιν.

Chapter 9 ⤳

1. ἄξιος γὰρ ὁ ἐργάτης τοῦ μισθοῦ αὐτοῦ. (Luke 10:7)
For the worker is worthy of his wage.

2. Ἀχιλεῦ, δάμαζε θυμὸν μέγαν. (Homer, *Iliad*)
Achilles, tame your great spirit.
- In Greek, the possessive is often omitted if the possessor is obvious from the context. Greek would say "The child loved the mother," where English would say "The child loved her mother." In this passage from Homer, the context of the poem makes it clear that the speaker, Phoenix, is talking about Achilles' *thumos*, and not someone else's *thumos*.

3. ἡ γὰρ σιωπὴ τοῖς σοφοῖσιν ἀπόκρισις. (Euripides, *Fragments*)
For silence is an answer for the wise.
For the wise, silence is an answer.
- Be sure that you are not translating γὰρ as "for" in "for the wise." γάρ is a conjunction, never a preposition. The "for" in "for the wise" is a translation of the dative of respect.

4. μὴ δίωκε τἀφανῆ. (Menander, Fragments)
Don't pursue unclear things.

5. πάντα στέγει, πάντα πιστεύει, πάντα ἐλπίζει, πάντα ὑπομένει. (1 Cor 13:7)
Love (ἀγάπη) sustains all things, trusts all things, hopes all things, endures all things.

6. ῥίζα γὰρ πάντων τῶν κακῶν ἐστιν ἡ φιλαργυρία. (1 Tim 6:10)
For love of money is the root of all evils.
- Literally "love of silver," but "love of money" conveys the sense of the word.

7. καλὸν ἀληθὴς καὶ ἀτενὴς παρρησία. (Euripides, *Fragments*)
True and earnest frankness is a beautiful thing.
- Greek will often use the neuter singular substantive adjective this way. ἀληθὴς and ἀτενὴς must modify παρρησία, not καλὸν, since they are feminine adjectives.

8. ἔστω δὲ ἡ προσποίησις τοῦ σωφρονεῖν ἀληθής. (Charondas, in Stobaeus, *Anthology*)
But let the claim of moderation be true.
- In such cases it is impossible to translate an articular infinite literally, hence the noun "moderation" is used to translate the genitive of the articular infinitive in this sentence.

9. ἡ παιδεία καθάπερ εὐδαίμων χώρα πάντα τὰ ἀγαθὰ φέρει. (Pythagoras, *Fragments*)
Education, just like a happy field, bears all good things.
Education, just like a fertile field, brings forth all good things.

10. μετὰ τὴν δόσιν τάχιστα γηράσκει χάρις. (Menander, *Fragments*)
A favor grows old quickly after the giving.
After it is given, a favor grows old quickly.
A favor, after it is given, is quickly forgotten.

Supplementary Exercises

Identify the declension of the following adjectives.

εὐδαίμων, –ον	3rd Declension
ἀληθής, –ές	3rd Declension
καλός, –ή, –όν	Adjective of the 1st and 2nd Declension
ἄξιος, –α, –ον	Adjective of the 1st and 2nd Declension
ἡδύς, ἡδεῖα, ἡδύ	Mixed Declension

Give the corresponding forms of the definite article and adjective for each of the following nouns.

Definite Article	Adjective ἀληθής	Definite	Adjective Article	εὐδαίμων	
τῷ	ἀληθεῖ	λόγῳ	ὁ	εὐδαίμων	Σωκράτης
ὁ	ἀληθής	δαίμων	τὰ	εὐδαίμονα	σώματα
τοῖς	ἀληθέσι	βιβλίοις	τὰς	εὐδαίμονας	ψυχάς
τοῦ	ἀληθοῦς	βασιλέως	οἱ	εὐδαίμονες	δαίμονες
τὴν	ἀληθῆ	πόλιν	τοῖς	εὐδαίμοσι	γένεσιν

Translate the following sentences into Greek.

γιγνώσκω = to know | εἰμί = to be | ἔχω = to have, hold | λέγω = to speak | πράττω = to do

1. The wife trusts the worthy husband.

ἡ γυνὴ πιστεύει τῷ ἀξίῳ ἀνδρί.

ἡ γυνὴ πιστεύει τῷ ἀνδρὶ τῷ ἀξίῳ.

2. The happy women speak true things.

αἱ εὐδαίμονες γυναῖκες λέγουσι τὰ ἀληθῆ.

3. I know the great temper of the man.

γιγνώσκω τὸν μέγαν θύμον τοῦ ἀνδρός.

τὸν μέγαν θύμον τοῦ ἀνδρὸς γιγνώσκω.

4. Let the women do great things.

πραττόντων αἱ γυναῖκες τὰ μεγάλα.

πραττόντων τὰ μεγάλα αἱ γυναῖκες.

5. A great spirit does many things.

ὁ μέγας θύμος πράττει τὰ πολλά.

6. All things are sweet to the happy man.

τὰ πάντα ἐστὶν ἡδέα τῷ εὐδαίμονι ἀνθρώπῳ.

πάντα ἐστὶν ἡδέα τῷ εὐδαίμονι ἀνδρί.

7. We trust the woman worthy of great things.

πιστεύομεν τὴν γυναῖκα τὴν ἀξίαν τῶν μεγάλων.

Chapter 10 ~

1. ὁ γὰρ πατὴρ φιλεῖ τὸν υἱὸν καὶ πάντα δείκνυσιν αὐτῷ ἃ αὐτὸς ποιεῖ. (John 5:20)

For the Father loves the son and reveals everything which he himself makes to him.

For the Father loves the son and shows to him all that he does.

- ποιέω means "to make," but it often has the meaning of "to do."
- While Classical Greek authors avoid the nominative of αὐτός when it is used as a personal pronoun, it occurs in Koine. This can make it difficult at times to distinguish it from the intensive use. Should this be translated as "which he does," or "which he himself does"? Sometimes it is difficult to choose one. Rarely does it dramatically change the meaning of the sentence, but it is something to be aware of.

2. ὃν γὰρ θεοὶ φιλοῦσιν ἀποθνήσκει νέος. (Menander, *Fragments*)

For he whom the gods love dies young.

- This sentence is tricky because of the placement of a relative without a stated antecedent. Most of the time this formulation begins with the nominative ὅς "he who. . . ". You will occasionally see this formulation used with other cases, as in the above example.
- Another difficulty with this sentence is the use of the adjective νέος, which is technically a subject complement.

3. εἰ δυνατόν ἐστιν, παρελθάτω ἀπ᾽ ἐμοῦ τὸ ποτήριον τοῦτο· πλὴν οὐχ ὡς ἐγὼ θέλω ἀλλ᾽ ὡς σύ. (Matt 26:39)

If it is possible, let this cup pass from me. But not as I wish but as you wish.

If it is possible, let this cup pass from me, but not as I will but as you will.

- Notice that the verb in ὡς σύ is implied. English is less inclined than Greek to have implied verbs. It is usually best, therefore, to add implied verbs in your translation if it would sound awkward otherwise.

4. τὸ γὰρ θανεῖν οὐκ αἰσχρόν, ἀλλ᾽ αἰσχρῶς θανεῖν. (Menander, *Fragments*)

For to die is not shameful, but to die shamefully is.

For dying is not shameful, but dying shamefully is.

5. ὁ μὲν ἀγαθὸς ἀνὴρ οὐκ εὐθέως εὐδαίμων ἐξ ἀνάγκης ἐστίν, ὁ δὲ εὐδαίμων καὶ ἀγαθὸς ἀνήρ ἐστιν. (Archytas, in Stobaeus, *Anthology*)

On the one hand, the good man is not simply happy by necessity, but, on the other hand, the happy man is by necessity also good.

The good man is not of necessity simply happy, but the happy man is necessarily also good.

- Just as in example three above, the implied εὐθέως in the second clause is best included in your translation.

6. ἕκαστος ἴδιον ἔχει χάρισμα ἐκ θεοῦ, ὁ μὲν οὕτως, ὁ δὲ οὕτως. (1 Cor 7:7)

Each has his own charism from God, one in this way, one in that way.

For each has his own gift from God, one in one way, one in another.

For each has his own gift from God, one has one gift, one has another.

7. ἔρως δίκαιος καρπὸν εὐθέως φέρει. (Menander, *Fragments*)

Just love bears fruit at once.

8. πᾶν τὸ κέρδος ἄδικον ὃ φέρει βλάβην. (Menander, *Fragments*)

Every gain is unjust which bears harm.

All profit which bears harm is unjust.

9. ἐγὼ βρῶσιν ἔχω φαγεῖν ἣν ὑμεῖς οὐκ οἴδατε. (John 4:32)

I have food to eat which you do not know.

10. καὶ αὐτός ἐστιν ἡ κεφαλὴ τοῦ σώματος, τῆς ἐκκλησίας· ὅς ἐστιν ἀρχή, πρωτότοκος ἐκ τῶν νεκρῶν. (Col 1:18)
And he is the head of the body, the church, (he) who is the beginning, the first born of the dead.

- English dislikes starting sentences with relative pronouns as subjects, so translators usually start a new sentence and translate the relative with a personal pronoun.
- If the context makes the meaning clear, you will see exceptions to the rule that the subject gets the article while the predicate nominative does not. The first half of this line is such an exception.

Supplementary Exercises

Convert the following adjectives into adverbs.

αἰσχρός	αἰσχρῶς	ἀληθής	ἀληθῶς
δυνατός	δυνατῶς	εὐδαίμων	εὐδαιμόνως
καλός	καλῶς		

Are the following words definite articles or relative pronouns?

οἵ	relative pronoun	ὅ	relative pronoun
οἱ	definite article	ὅς	relative pronoun
αἱ	definite article	τά	definite article
αἵ	relative pronoun	ἅ	relative pronoun
τό	definite article	ὧν	relative pronoun

Translate the following sentences into Greek.
γιγνώσκω = to know | εἰμί = to be | λέγω = to speak

1. The beginning of love is strong.
ἡ ἀρχὴ τοῦ ἔρωτός ἐστι δυνατή.

2. Let the church not do shameful things.
ἡ ἐκκλησία μὴ πραττέτω τὰ αἰσχρά.
μὴ πραττέτω ἡ ἐκκλησία τὰ αἰσχρά.

3. The church is now young, but she is strong.
ἡ μὲν ἐκκλησία νῦν νέα ἐστί, δυνατὴ δέ.

4. Let each person who is young always know love.
ἕκαστος ὅς ἐστι νέος ἀεὶ γιγνωσκέτω τὸν ἔρωτα.

5. The young men are always speaking to the shameful man whom I know.
οἱ νεανίαι ἀεὶ λέγουσι τῷ αἰσχρῷ ἀνδρὶ ὅν γιγνώσκω.

6. You (singular) know the beginning of love, which has profit.
γιγνώσκεις τὴν ἀρχὴν τοῦ ἔρωτος, ὃ ἔχει κέρδος.
    * The neuter ὃ is here used because that which has profit is the previous clause, the fact that one knows the beginning of love. If it was love which has profit, ὃς would have been used instead of ὃ.

Chapter 11 ～

1. ὁ παιδείας ἀμύητος πῶς ἄλλους ἀνθρώπους παιδεύσει. (Aesop, *Fables*)
How will the one uninitiated in education educate other people?
How will the uneducated one teach others?
The one uninitiated in education, how will he educate other men?

2. κἀγὼ δέ σοι λέγω ὅτι σὺ εἶ Πέτρος, καὶ ἐπὶ ταύτῃ τῇ πέτρᾳ οἰκοδομήσω μου τὴν ἐκκλησίαν, καὶ πύλαι ᾄδου οὐ κατισχύσουσιν αὐτῆς. (Matthew 16:18)
And I say to you that you are Peter, and upon this rock I will build my Church, and the gates of hell (literally 'gates of Hades') will not overpower it.
And I say to you, "You are Peter, and upon this rock I will build my Church, and the gates of hell will not overpower her.

- Occasionally in Koine, ὅτι is used to introduce quotations and is not translated. I would, however, suggest only leaving ὅτι untranslated if it sounds awkward.
- Some prefer to translate the pronoun αὐτῆς as "it," while others prefer "her." Most of the time translating the gender of pronouns is a mistake, since the English words to which they refer don't have gender. There are exceptions. English uses feminine pronouns to refer to ships, and the Church, frequently called the bride of Christ, is often referred to with the feminine pronoun.

3. οἴδαμεν δὲ ὅτι τοῖς ἀγαπῶσιν τὸν θεὸν πάντα συνεργεῖ εἰς ἀγαθόν. (Rom 8:28)
And we know that for those loving God, all things work together for good.

- δὲ will sometimes be translated as "but," and sometimes as "and." It depends on the context. Since you are dealing with isolated sentences in this book, try "but," and when that doesn't work, try "and." Don't be too concerned with which one is correct. When you read continuous Greek, it will become apparent.

4. νόμιζε τοὺς ἀληθινοὺς φίλους εἶναι ἀδελφούς. (Menander, *Fragments*)
Consider true friends to be brothers.
Think that true friends are brothers.

- While occasionally it works to translate an indirect statement literally, as in the first example, the majority of Greek verbs that take indirect statement won't translate literally. It is for this reason that I suggest you add the word "that" into your indirect statements and translate the infinitive as a finite verb. Even though I always err on the side of "the more literal the better," I think indirect statement is an exception.
- Notice which of the nouns has the definite article. Hence it would be incorrect to say "Think that brothers are true friends."

5. ἄξεις ἀλύπως τὸν βίον χωρὶς γάμου. (Menander, *Fragments*)
You will live life painlessly without marriage.

- While ἀλύπως is technically an adverb, often Greek uses adverbs where English prefers an adjective, and vice versa. It will not be incorrect to say "You will lead a painless life," as long as you understand it is an adverb.

6. ἕκαστος γὰρ τὸ ἴδιον φορτίον βαστάσει. (Gal 6:5)
For each one will bear his own burden.
For each person will carry his own burden.

7. θεὸν σέβου καὶ πάντα πράξεις εὐθέως. (Menander, *Fragments*)
Worship god and you will do everything correctly.
Revere a god and you will do all things correctly.
Revere the god and you will do all things correctly.

- When classical Greek uses θεός in the singular, it can be difficult to know whether to use a definite article, an indefinite article, or if you should leave out an article. The more context you have, the better. In fragments, this will often present a difficulty.

8. ἀλλά σ' ἐς Ἠλύσιον πεδίον καὶ πείρατα γαίης ἀθάνατοι πέμψουσιν. (Homer, *Odyssey*)
But the immortals will send you to the Elysian field and the ends of the earth.
But the immortal gods will send you to the Elysian field and the ends of the earth.

9. ἀλλὰ μάτην ὁ πρόθυμος ἀεὶ πόνον ἕξει. (Euripides, *Children of Heracles*)
But in vain the eager person will always have toil.
But in vain the eager man will always have toil.

10. πολλαὶ μέν ἐσμεν, λέξομεν δὲ συντόμως. (Aeschylus, *Eumenides*)
On the one hand we are many, but we will speak concisely.
Although we are many, we will speak briefly.
- While I suggest using "on the one hand . . . on the other hand" in the beginning to make sure you know the character of the construction, it sounds awkward and can be discarded once you are comfortable with μέν δέ constructions.

Supplementary Exercises

Change the following present indicative forms into the corresponding forms of the future indicative.

Present	Future	Present	Future
Indicative	Indicative	Indicative	Indicative
λύω	λύσω	πέμπεις	πέμψεις
λύετε	λύσετε	ἄγει	ἄξει
πέμπουσιν	πέμψουσιν	ἄγομεν	ἄξομεν

Change the following direct statements into indirect statements with ὅτι, introduced by Σωκράτης λέγει "Socrates says that…"

1. ἡ γῆ ἐστι πέτρα.
Σωκράτης λέγει ὅτι ἡ γῆ ἐστι πέτρα.
2. ὁ ἀδελφὸς οὐκ ἔστιν ἀληθινός.
Σωκράτης λέγει ὅτι ὁ ἀδελφὸς οὐκ ἔστιν ἀληθινός.
3. οἱ ἄλλοι ἄγουσι τοὺς ἀληθινοὺς ἀδελφούς.
Σωκράτης λέγει ὅτι οἱ ἄλλοι ἄγουσι τοὺς ἀληθινοὺς ἀδελφούς.
4. οἱ ἄλλοι οὐ λέγουσι τὰ ἀληθινά.
Σωκράτης λέγει ὅτι οἱ ἄλλοι οὐ λέγουσι τὰ ἀληθινά.

Change the following direct statements into indirect statements with the accusative and infinitive, introduced by Σωκράτης φησὶ "Socrates says that…"

1. ἡ γῆ ἐστι πέτρα.
Σωκράτης φησὶ τὴν γῆν εἶναι πέτραν.
2. ὁ ἀδελφὸς οὐκ ἔστιν ἀληθινός.
Σωκράτης φησὶ τὸν ἀδελφὸν οὐκ εἶναι ἀληθινόν.
3. οἱ ἄλλοι ἄγουσι τοὺς ἀληθινοὺς ἀδελφούς.
Σωκράτης φησὶ τοὺς ἄλλους ἄγειν τοὺς ἀληθινοὺς ἀδελφούς.
4. οἱ ἄλλοι οὐ λέγουσι τὰ ἀληθινά.
Σωκράτης φησὶ τοὺς ἄλλους οὐ λέγειν τὰ ἀληθινά.

Translate the following sentences into Greek.
❡ ἄνθρωπος, –ου, ὁ = human being, person | γιγνώσκω = to know | εἰμί = to be | κακός, –ή, –όν (adj.) = bad, base, evil | λέγω = to speak

1. Socrates says that the bad people lead trustful people to Hades.
ὁ Σωκράτης λέγει ὅτι οἱ κακοὶ ἄνθρωποι ἄγουσι τοὺς ἀληθινοὺς ἀνθρώπους εἰς ᾅδην.
ὁ Σωκράτης φησὶ τοὺς κακοὺς ἀνθρώπους ἄγειν τοὺς ἀληθινοὺς ἀνθρώπους εἰς ᾅδην.

- For the most part, when the author views the speech as an opinion or belief, the accusative and infinitive construction is preferred. The line between reported speech and opinion is vague at best, and you will often see ὅτι used to express opinions. Likewise, while λέγω tends to be used with the ὅτι construction and φημί with the accusative + infinitive construction, there are exceptions.

2. Socrates thinks that the earth is a rock.
ὁ Σωκράτης νομίζει τὴν γῆν εἶναι πέτραν.

3. The evil brother will send the trustful brother to the gate.
ὁ κακὸς ἀδελφὸς ἄξει τὸν ἀληθινὸν ἀδελφὸν εἰς τὴν πύλην.

4. Let the evil man know Hades.
ὁ κακὸς ἄνθρωπος γιγνωσκέτω τὴν ᾅδην.
γιγνωσκέτω τὴν ᾅδην ὁ κακὸς ἄνθρωπος.

5. You (plural) will know the trustful brother.
γνώσεσθε τὸν ἀληθινὸν ἀδελφόν.
  - There was an error in the making of this exercise. The author forgot that the future of γιγνώσκω was deponent, a type of verb not introduced until chapter 15.

Chapter 12 ~

1. ἐν ἀρχῇ ἦν ὁ λόγος, καὶ ὁ λόγος ἦν πρὸς τὸν θεόν, καὶ θεὸς ἦν ὁ λόγος.
(John 1:1)
In the beginning was the Word, and the Word was towards God, and the Word was God.
In the beginning was the Word, and the Word was with God, and the Word was God.
In the beginning was the Word, and the Word was facing God, and the Word was God.

2. χαλεπὸν τὸ εὖ γνῶναι. (Pittacus, in Stobaeus, *Anthology*)
To know well is difficult.
It is difficult to understand well.
Knowing well is difficult.
  • Articular infinitives are verbal nouns. While the definite article can never be translated, I prefer to keep the infinitive translation, as in the first example, especially for beginning students.

3. Λακεδαιμόνιοι τριακοσίους εἰς Θερμοπύλας ἔπεμψαν. (Stobaeus, *Anthology*)
The Lacedaemonians sent 300 soldiers to Thermopylae.
The Spartans sent 300 men to Thermopylae.

4. ἡ γλῶσσα πολλοὺς εἰς ὄλεθρον ἤγαγεν. (Menander, *Fragments*)
The tongue led many to destruction.
The tongue led many people to ruin.

5. οὐχὶ ἐμώρανεν ὁ θεὸς τὴν σοφίαν τοῦ κόσμου; (1 Cor 1:20)·

Do you not know that God made foolish the wisdom of the world?

Do you not know that God has made foolish the wisdom of the world?

- In Koine you will often see the aorist tense used where classical Greek would use the perfect tense.

6. ἑκάστῳ ὡς ὁ θεὸς ἐμέρισεν μέτρον πίστεως, (Rom 12:3)

As God apportioned a measure of faith to each.

As to each God has apportioned a measure of the faith.

(reading this sentence as a continuation of the previous clause) ... to each as God has appointed a measure of faith.

7. ἐξομολογοῦμαί σοι, πάτερ, κύριε τοῦ οὐρανοῦ καὶ τῆς γῆς, ὅτι ἀπέκρυψας ταῦτα ἀπὸ σοφῶν καὶ συνετῶν, καὶ ἀπεκάλυψας αὐτὰ νηπίοις. (Luke 10:21)

I give you thanks, Father, Lord of heaven and earth, because you hid these things from the wise and intelligent, and you revealed them to the children.

I give you thanks, Father, Lord of heaven and earth, that you have hidden these things from the wise and clever, and you have revealed them to the childlike.

- See note to sentence 5 above.

8. ἡ πολλῶν ἀνδρῶν γόνατ᾽ ἔλυσε. (Homer, *Odyssey*)

She (Helen) loosened the knees of many men.

She weakened the knees of many men.

- Often soldiers are described as being weak in the knees when terrified in battle. Homer is comparing Helen's beauty to the fear a warrior could impress on his enemies.

9. ἡμεῖς δὲ οὐ τὸ πνεῦμα τοῦ κόσμου ἐλάβομεν ἀλλὰ τὸ πνεῦμα τὸ ἐκ τοῦ θεοῦ. (1 Cor 2:12)

But we did not receive the spirit of the world, but the spirit from God.

But we have not received the spirit of the world, but the spirit of God.

10. ἔστω δὲ πᾶς ἄνθρωπος ταχὺς εἰς τὸ ἀκοῦσαι, βραδὺς εἰς τὸ λαλῆσαι, βραδὺς εἰς ὀργήν. (James 1:19)

But let every man be quick to hear, slow to speak, slow to anger.
And let everyone be quick to hear, slow to speak, slow to anger.

Supplementary Exercises

Change the following present indicative forms into the corresponding
forms of the imperfect and aorist indicative.

Present Indicative	Imperfect Indicative	Aorist Indicative
λύω	ἔλυον	ἔλυσα
ἀποκρύπτεις	ἀπέκρυπτες	ἀπέκρυψας
ἀκούει	ἤκουε[ν]	ἤκουσα
ἀποκαλύπτομεν	ἀπεκαλύπτομεν	ἀπεκαλύψαμεν
λαμβάνετε	ἐλαμβάνετε	ἐλάβετε
μερίζουσιν	ἐμέριζον	ἐμέρισαν

Change the following forms of the present imperative into the corresponding forms of the aorist imperative.

Present Imperative	Aorist Imperative	Present Imperative	Aorist Imperative
λῦε	λῦσον	λαμβάνετε	λάβετε
λυόντων	λυσάντων	μεριζόντων	μερισάντων
ἀκουέτω	ἀκουσάτω	ἀπόκρυπτε	ἀπόκρυψον

Change the following forms of the present indicative of εἰμί into the corresponding forms of the imperfect indicative.

εἰμί	ἦ or ἦν	εἶ	ἦσθα
ἐστί	ἦν	ἐσμέν	ἦμεν
ἐστέ	ἦτε or ἦστε	εἰσίν	ἦσαν

Translate the following sentences into Greek.

¶ ἄνθρωπος, –ου, ὁ = human being, person | κακός, –ή, –όν (adj.) = bad, base, evil

1. The spirit seized the person.

τὸ πνεῦμα ἔλαβε τὸν ἄνθρωπον.

2. The quick person was seizing the slow person.

ὁ ταχὺς ἄνθρωπος ἐλάμβανε τὸν βραδὺν ἄνθρωπον.

ὁ ἄνθρωπος ὁ ταχὺς ἐλάμβανε τὸν ἄνθρωπον τὸν βραδύν.

3. We do not hear the childish language.

οὐκ ἀκούομεν τὴν νηπίαν γλῶτταν (γλῶσσαν).

  • Remember that in Koine, ττ becomes σσ.

4. We do not hear the childish person.

οὐκ ἀκούομεν τὸν νηπίον ἄνθρωπον.

5. Seize (singular) the knees of the swift person.

λάβε τὰ γόνατα τοῦ ταχέος ἀνθρώπου.

6. Seize (singular) the knees of the swift person (and don't let go).

λάμβανε τὰ γόνατα τοῦ ταχέος ἀνθρώπου.

  • Notice the use of the present imperative here as opposed to the aorist imperative above.

7. The heavens hear the language of the children.

οἱ οὐρανοὶ ἀκούουσι τὴν γλῶτταν (γλῶσσαν) τῶν νηπίων.

  • The genitive plural of other words for children are of course acceptable here.

8. The heavens heard the children.

οἱ οὐρανοὶ ἤκουσαν τοὺς νηπίους.

9. Let the child reveal the spirit.

ὁ νήπιος ἀποκαλυψάτω τὸ πνεῦμα.

ἀποκαλυψάτω ὁ νήπιος τὸ πνεῦμα.

Chapter 13 ~

1. τῇ νυκτὶ βουλὴ τοῖς σοφοῖσι γίγνεται. (Menander, *Fragments*)
Counsel happens to the wise at night.
Counsel comes to the wise at night.
- γίγνωμαι can often be difficult to translate literally.

2. ἔπειτα μετὰ τρία ἔτη ἀνῆλθον εἰς Ἱεροσόλυμα ἱστορῆσαι Κηφᾶν, καὶ ἐπέμεινα πρὸς αὐτὸν ἡμέρας δεκαπέντε. (Gal 1:18)
Then after three years I went up to Jerusalem to visit Cephas (Peter), and I remained with him 15 days.

3. φιλοσοφίαν πρῶτος ὠνόμασε Πυθαγόρας καὶ ἑαυτὸν φιλόσοφον, μηδένα γὰρ ἔλεγεν εἶναι σοφὸν ἀλλὰ θεόν. (Diogenes Laertius, *Lives of Eminent Philosophers*)
Pythagoras first named philosophy and himself a philosopher. For he used to say that no one is wise but god.
Pythagoras first coined the term philosophy and called himself a philosopher. For he said that no one was wise but god.
- Remember that while the Greek is simple, sometimes it can be difficult to render into English an indirect statement introduced by a past tense verb. English normally would change the verb into the past, "was wise," but since it is a universal statement "is wise" is also permissible.

4. τῆς παιδείας ἔφη τὰς μὲν ῥίζας εἶναι πικράς, τὸν δὲ καρπὸν γλυκύν. (Aristotle, in Diogenes Laertius, *Lives of Eminent Philosophers*)
He (Aristotle) said that the roots of education are bitter, but the fruit is sweet.

5. οὐ πιστεύεις ὅτι ἐγὼ ἐν τῷ πατρὶ καὶ ὁ πατὴρ ἐν ἐμοί ἐστιν; τὰ ῥήματα ἃ ἐγὼ λαλῶ ὑμῖν ἀπ᾿ ἐμαυτοῦ οὐ λαλῶ· ὁ δὲ πατὴρ ἐν ἐμοὶ μένων ποιεῖ τὰ ἔργα αὐτοῦ. (John 14:10)

Do you not believe that I am in the Father and the Father is in me? The words which I speak to you I do not speak from myself, but the Father remaining in me does his works.

6. ἐν ἐκείνῃ τῇ ἡμέρᾳ γνώσεσθε ὑμεῖς ὅτι ἐγὼ ἐν τῷ πατρί μου καὶ ὑμεῖς ἐν ἐμοὶ κἀγὼ ἐν ὑμῖν. (John 14:20)

On that day you will know that I am in my father and you are in me and I in you.

7. καὶ ἰδοὺ ἐγὼ μεθ᾿ ὑμῶν εἰμι πάσας τὰς ἡμέρας ἕως τῆς συντελείας τοῦ αἰῶνος. (Matt 28:20)

And behold, I am with you all the days until the end of the age.

- Behold is how ἰδοὺ is traditionally translated, but "look" or "see" are suitable translations as well. ἰδοὺ is normally the Greek translation of the Hebrew word הִנֵּה, which can be a bit tricky to translate. It signals that something important is about to be said. Some translators of Hebrew even think it should be left untranslated.
- Notice the accusative of duration of time.

8. ἦν δὲ ἄνθρωπος ἐκ τῶν Φαρισαίων, Νικόδημος ὄνομα αὐτῷ, ἄρχων τῶν Ἰουδαίων· οὗτος ἦλθεν πρὸς αὐτὸν νυκτὸς καὶ εἶπεν αὐτῷ, "Ῥαββί, οἴδαμεν ὅτι ἀπὸ θεοῦ ἐλήλυθας διδάσκαλος." (John 3:1–2)

There was a man of the Pharisees, whose name was Nicodemus, a leader of the Jews. This one came to him during the night and said to him "Rabbi, we know that you have come as a teacher from God."

- Notice the genitive of time within which.
- When Greek uses nominatives with 1st and 2nd person verbs, it is sometimes best to add "as a. . . ," since "you, a teacher, have come. . ." can sound a bit odd.

9. τὸ γὰρ ἅγιον πνεῦμα διδάξει ὑμᾶς ἐν αὐτῇ τῇ ὥρᾳ ἃ δεῖ εἰπεῖν. (Luke 12:12)

For the Holy Spirit will teach you on that very day all the things which are necessary to say.

- Notice the intensive use of αὐτῇ in this sentence.
- Notice how the word "things" is missing. Only the relative pronoun ἃ "which" is in the sentence. The antecedent is missing, but we usually add it back in the English translation. This suppression of the antecedent is quite common in Greek.

10. ὁ Ἀναξαγόρας ἔλεγεν ὅτι ἡ σελήνη ἀπὸ τοῦ ἡλίου ἔχει τὸ φῶς. (Socrates, in Plato, *Cratylus*)
Anaxagoras used to say that the moon holds light from the sun.
Anaxagoras said that the moon gets its light from the sun.

- Very often in Greek, when the possessor is obvious, a possessive adjective or pronoun is not needed. You will often, however, choose to add it back in your English translation, as in the second example.

Supplementary Exercises

Change the present tense verb that introduces the following indirect statements into the future and translate.
❡ ἄνθρωπος, –ου, ὁ = human being | νομίζω, νομιῶ = to think, consider (the 3rd singular future of νομίζω is νομιεῖ)

1. Σωκράτης λέγει ὅτι ἡ φιλοσοφία διδάσκει τοὺς ἀνθρώπους.
Σωκράτης λέξει ὅτι ἡ φιλοσοφία διδάσκει τοὺς ἀνθρώπους.

2. Σωκράτης νομίζει τὸ φῶς εἶναι ἅγιον.
Σωκράτης νομιεῖ τὸ φῶς εἶναι ἅγιον.

Change the present tense verb that introduces the following indirect statements into the aorist and translate.
1. Σωκράτης λέγει ὅτι ἡ φιλοσοφία διδάσκει τοὺς ἀνθρώπους.
Σωκράτης εἶπεν ὅτι ἡ φιλοσοφία διδάσκει τοὺς ἀνθρώπους.

2. Σωκράτης νομίζει τὸ φῶς εἶναι ἅγιον.

Σωκράτης ἐνόμισε τὸ φῶς εἶναι ἅγιον.

Indicate whether each of the following English sentences would be expressed with a Greek (1) genitive of time within which, (2) accusative of duration of time, or (3) dative of time when.

1. The students slept throughout   *Accusative of Duration of Time*
   the lecture.
2. The students laughed during   *Genitive of Time Within Which*
   the lecture.
3. The students slept at the lecture.   *Dative of Time When*

Translate the following sentences into Greek.

❡ ἄνθρωπος, –ου, ὁ = human being, person | κακός, –ή, –όν (adj.) = bad, base, evil | λέγω = to say, speak

1. We used to speak to the philosopher.

ἐλέγομεν τῷ φιλοσόφῳ.

2. We spoke to the philosopher.

εἴπομεν τῷ φιλοσόφῳ.

ἐλέξαμεν τῷ φιλοσόφῳ.

- The first aorist of λέγω, ἔλεξα, while technically correct, is very rarely used. For the aorist of λέγω, use the 2nd aorist εἶπον instead.

3. I used to call the counsel of the philosopher evil.

ὠνόμαζον τὴν βουλὴν τοῦ φιλοσόφου κακήν.

ὠνόμαζον τὴν τοῦ φιλοσόφου βουλὴν κακήν.

4. I called the counsel of the philosopher evil.

ὠνόμασα τὴν βουλὴν τοῦ φιλοσόφου κακήν.

ὠνόμασα τὴν τοῦ φιλοσόφου βουλὴν κακήν.

5. You (plural) said that you had taught the philosopher.

εἴπετε ὅτι ἐδίδαξας τὸν φιλόσοφον.

6. You (plural) said that you were teaching the philosopher.

εἴπετε ὅτι διδάσκεις τὸν φιλόσοφον.

- Remember that it is only in English that we must change the verb of the indirect statement if it is introduced by a past tense verb. The Greek is simple: retain the original tense of the indirect statement.

7. The philosophers call the day night.

οἱ φιλόσοφοι ὀνομάζουσι τὴν ἡμέραν νύκτα.

8. I say that the philosophers will speak to the evil people.

λέγω ὅτι οἱ φιλόσοφοι λέξουσι τοῖς κακοῖς ἀνθρώποις.

9. I said that the philosophers would speak to the evil people.

εἶπον ὅτι οἱ φιλόσοφοι λέξουσι τοῖς κακοῖς ἀνθρώποις.

Chapter 14 ～

1. καὶ μὴ συσχηματίζεσθε τῷ αἰῶνι τούτῳ, ἀλλὰ μεταμορφοῦσθε τῇ ἀνακαινώσει τοῦ νοός. (Rom 12:2)
Do not conform to this age, but be transformed by the renewal of the mind.
Do not conform to this age, but be transformed by the renewal of your mind.
   - When the possessor is obvious, Greek does not need to state it. English, on the other hand, prefers to include a possessive adjective or pronoun, even when it is obvious. You may wish to add a possessive from time to time, as in the second translation above.
Don't be conformed by this age, but be transformed by the renewal of your mind.
   - Since the middle and passive imperatives are identical in spelling, one can make a case for either translation.
   - The datives in both of these cases could be interpreted as datives of respect, or datives of means (chapter 24).

2. ὁ ἄνθρωπος ἀτυχῶν σῴζεται ὑπὸ τῆς ἐλπίδος. (Menander, *Fragments*)
The unlucky man is saved by hope.

3. ἀρκεῖ σοι ἡ χάρις μου· ἡ γὰρ δύναμις ἐν ἀσθενείᾳ τελεῖται. (2 Cor 12:9)
My grace suffices for you. For power is perfected in weakness.
My grace is enough for you. For power is perfected in weakness.
   - While it is fine, and occasionally necessary, to translate Greek verbs with a verb of "to be" and an adjective, I am generally not a fan of this for beginning students. When possible, choose the first trans-

lation rather than the second. I generally prefer beginning students keep verbs verbs and adjectives adjectives. This helps prevent you from "getting the gist of it" and guessing. Once you become more proficient in your command of Greek, you can afford to have more leeway in translations without the risk of developing bad habits.

4. τὸ δὲ παιδίον ηὔξανεν καὶ ἐκραταιοῦτο πληρούμενον σοφίᾳ, καὶ χάρις θεοῦ ἦν ἐπ' αὐτό. (Luke 2:40)
And the child grew and became strong, filled with wisdom, and the grace of God was upon him.

5. πείθεται γὰρ τὸ πλῆθος τοῖς δημαγωγοῖς. (Aristotle, *Politics*)
For the multitude obeys demagogues.
- It wouldn't be necessarily wrong to translate this as "The multitude is persuaded by demagogues." The middle and passive are identical in spelling, but the more natural construction with passive verbs is the genitive of agent. It is for this reason that I favor reading πείθεται as middle rather than passive.

6. καὶ εἰς ἐπιθυμίας αἰσχρὰς καὶ ψυχοβλαβεῖς μὴ τρέπεσθε, ἀλλ' ὁλοψύχως τὰς ἐντολὰς τοῦ Θεοῦ φυλάξατε. (John Chrysostom, *Sermons*)
Do not turn to shameful and soul-destroying desires, but with all your soul keep the commandments of God.

7. ὁ γέρων πάμπρωτος ὑφαίνειν ἤρχετο μῆτιν Νέστωρ. (Homer, *Iliad*)
The old man Nestor first of all began to weave his plan.
- See first note on sentence one for the inclusion of "his" to this translation.
- Notice how Nestor is the final word of the sentence. This is quite common in Homer. Almost all the names of the heroes and gods are capable of metrically closing a line in dactylic hexameter.

8. ἄρχεται δὲ ὁ πόλεμος ἐνθένδε ἤδη Ἀθηναίων καὶ Πελοποννησίων καὶ τῶν ἑκατέροις συμμάχων. (Thucydides, *History of the Peloponnesian War*)

And now really began the war between the Athenians and Peloponnesians and their allies.

- Notice the emphatic placement of ἄρχεται at the start of the sentence.
- While the English "their" is ambiguous, the Greek makes it clear that the "allies" refer to the allies of both the Athenians and Peloponnesians.

9. ὑφ᾿ ἡδονῆς ὁ φρόνιμος οὐχ ἁλίσκεται. (Menander, *Fragments*)
The prudent man is not caught by pleasure.
The prudent person does not succumb to pleasure.

10. ὁ Σωκράτης οὔτε πείθεται οὔτε πείθει ἡμᾶς. (Plato, *Crito*)
Socrates is neither persuaded nor persuades us.
Socrates neither obeys nor persuades us.

- πείθεται could be read as a middle or passive verb.
- The "by us" of the first translation and the "us" of the second translation are implied.

Supplementary Exercises

Give the corresponding middle/passive forms for the following active forms.

Active	Middle/Passive	Active	Middle/Passive
ἔλυον (1st person sing.)	ἐλυόμην	λύομεν	λυόμεθα
ἔλυον (3rd person pl.)	ἐλύοντο	λῦε	λύου
λύει	λύεται	λύειν	λύεσθαι

Switch the following sentences from active constructions into passive constructions with a genitive of agent. For example, for ἡ δύναμις πείθει ἀσθένειαν "Power persuades weakness," write ἡ ἀσθένεια πείθεται ὑπὸ δυνάμεως "Weakness is persuaded by power."

§ ἄνθρωπος, –ου, ὁ = human being, γιγνώσκω = to know

1. τὸ πλῆθος φυλάττει τὸ παιδίον.
τὸ παιδίον φυλάττεται ὑπὸ τοῦ πλήθους.

2. ὁ νοῦς γιγνώσκει δύναμιν.
ἡ δύναμις γιγνώσκεται ὑπὸ τοῦ νοῦ.

3. οἱ ἄνθρωποι ἔσωζον τὸ παιδίον.
τὸ παιδίον ἐσώζετο ὑπὸ τῶν ἀνθρώπων.

4. ἐφυλάττομεν τὰ παιδία.
τὰ παιδία ἐσώζοντο ὑφ᾿ ἡμῶν.
   • ὑπὸ is changed to ὑπ᾿ before words that begin with a vowel with
     smooth breathing, ὑφ᾿ before words that begin with a vowel with
     rough breathing.

5. ὁ πόλεμος ἄρχει τῶν ἀνθρώπων.
οἱ ἄνθρωποι ἄρχονται ὑπὸ τοῦ πολέμου.

Translate the following sentences into Greek.
❡ ἄνθρωπος, –ου, ὁ = human being, person | κακός, –ή, –όν (adj.) = bad,
base, evil | πάλιν (adv.) = back, again

1. Don't (plural) turn back.
μὴ τρέπεσθε πάλιν.

2. The children did not obey the base people.
τὰ παιδία οὐκ ἐπείθοντο τοῖς κακοῖς ἀνθρώποις.

3. The mind is on guard against weakness.
ὁ νοῦς φυλάττεται τὴν ἀσθένειαν.
ὁ νοῦς φυλάσσεται τὴν ἀσθένειαν.

4. The multitude obeys power.
τὸ πλῆθος πείθεται τῇ δυνάμει.

5. The multitude are persuaded by power.
τὸ πλῆθος πείθεται ὑπὸ τῆς δυνάμεως.

Chapter 15 ～

1. ὡς μὲν βούλομαι, οὐ δύναμαι· ὡς δὲ δύναμαι, οὐ βούλομαι. (Theocritus, in Stobaeus, *Anthology*)

As I want, I am not able, and as I am able, I do not want.

I am not able (to write prose) as I wish, and I do not wish (to write prose) as I am able to.

2. ἔρχεσθε καὶ ὄψεσθε. (John 1:39)

Come and you will see.

- The famous line "Come and see," which uses two imperatives, is from verse 46 of this chapter, but is spoken by Philip to Nathaniel. Note that while ἔρχεσθε is imperative, ὄψεσθε is future indicative.

3. φιλόπονος ἴσθι καὶ βίον κτήσῃ καλόν. (Menander, *Fragments*)

Be industrious and you will have a beautiful life.

Be industrious and you will have a fine life.

Be a lover of hard work and you will have a noble life.

- Notice how the key words, the adjectives φιλόπονος and καλόν, are placed first and last in the sentence.

4. διὰ τὸ θαυμάζειν οἱ ἄνθρωποι καὶ νῦν καὶ τὸ πρῶτον ἤρξαντο φιλοσοφεῖν. (Aristotle, *Metaphysics*)

On account of wonder people both now and previously began to philosophize.

- It is almost impossible to translate articular infinitives literally. Sometimes the English gerund (wondering) works best, and sometimes a simple noun (wonder) will suffice.

5. καὶ ὁ λόγος σὰρξ ἐγένετο καὶ ἐσκήνωσεν ἐν ἡμῖν. (John 1:14)

And the word became flesh and dwelled among us.

And the word became flesh and pitched a tent among us.

And the word became flesh and tabernacled among us.

- The second translation is the most literal, as the verb comes from the noun σκηνή, which means "tent."

6. ὀργὴ γὰρ ἀνδρὸς δικαιοσύνην θεοῦ οὐκ ἐργάζεται. (James 1:20)

For the anger of man does not accomplish the righteousness of God.

For the anger of man does not produce the justice of God.

7. βουλόμεθα πλουτεῖν πάντες, ἀλλ᾽ οὐ δυνάμεθα. (Menander, *Fragments*)

We all want to be rich, but we are not able.

We all want, but are not able, to be rich.

8. πάτερ, εἰ βούλει παρένεγκε τοῦτο τὸ ποτήριον ἀπ᾽ ἐμοῦ· πλὴν μὴ τὸ θέλημά μου ἀλλὰ τὸ σὸν γινέσθω. (Luke 22:42)

Father, if you are willing, turn aside this cup from me, but may not my will but yours happen.

Father, if you are willing, turn aside this cup from me, but let your will, not mine, happen.

- παρένεγκε is a 2nd person imperative. The common translation "let this cup pass from me" is from Matthew 26:39, which uses a 3rd person imperative.

9. ἐνδύσασθε οὖν ὡς ἐκλεκτοὶ τοῦ θεοῦ, ἅγιοι καὶ ἠγαπημένοι, σπλάγχνα οἰκτιρμοῦ, χρηστότητα, ταπεινοφροσύνην, πραΰτητα, μακροθυμίαν. (Col 3:12)

Therefore, as chosen people of God, holy and beloved, put on the innards of compassion, goodness, humility, gentleness, and patience.

Therefore, as chosen people of God, holy and beloved, put on the heart of compassion, goodness, humility, gentleness, and patience.

- The literal translation of σπλάγχνα, "innards," or "bowels," sounds terrible in English, so some other way is necessary. Since it denotes the seat of emotions, "heart" is a common English translation.

10. ἐν ἀρχῇ ἦν ὁ λόγος, καὶ ὁ λόγος ἦν πρὸς τὸν θεόν, καὶ θεὸς ἦν ὁ λόγος. οὗτος ἦν ἐν ἀρχῇ πρὸς τὸν θεόν. πάντα δι᾽ αὐτοῦ ἐγένετο, καὶ χωρὶς αὐτοῦ ἐγένετο οὐδὲ ἕν. (John 1:1–3)
In the beginning was the Word, and the Word was with God, and the Word was God. This one (the Word) was in the beginning with God. Through him all things came to be, and apart from him nothing (came to be).
In the beginning was the Word, and the Word was with God, and the Word was God. This one (the Word) was in the beginning with God. Through him all things came to be, and not one thing (came to be) apart from him.

- Since there were no spaces between letters, sometimes a manuscript has οὐδὲ ἕν, "not one thing," and sometimes οὐδὲν, "nothing."

Supplementary Exercises

Change the following aorist active imperatives into aorist middle imperatives.

Aorist Active Imperative	Aorist Middle Imperative	Aorist Active Imperative	Aorist Middle Imperative
λῦσον	λῦσαι	λυσάντων	λυσάσθων
λύσατε	λύσασθε	λυσάτω	λυσάσθω

Change the following present middle/passive imperatives into aorist middle imperatives.

Present Middle/ Passive Imperative	Aorist Middle Imperative	Present Middle/ Passive Imperative	Aorist Middle Imperative
λυέσθων	λυσάσθων	λύεσθε	λύσασθε
λυέσθω	λυσάσθω	λύου	λῦσαι

Change the following present indicative forms of εἰμί into future indicatives.

Present Indicative	Future Indicative	Present Indicative	Future Indicative
εἰμί	ἔσομαι	ἐστέ	ἔσεσθε
ἐστίν	ἔσται	ἐσμέν	ἐσόμεθα
εἶ	ἔσῃ (ἔσει)	εἰσί	ἔσονται

Translate the following sentences into Greek.

¶ ἀνήρ, ανδρός, ὁ = man, husband | γυνή, γυναικός, ἡ = woman; wife | εὐδαίμων, –ον (adj.) = fortunate, happy

1. We don't want to go.
οὐ βουλόμεθα ἐλθεῖν.

2. Let your will come to be.
τὸ σὸν θέλημα γινέσθω.
γινέσθω τὸ θέλημά σου.
Greek will often use a genitive of possession with a pronoun rather than a possessive adjective.

3. Justice will come.
ἡ δικαιοσύνη ἐλεύσεται.
ἡ δίκη ἐλεύσεται.

4. The men will be able to marvel.
οἱ ἄνθρωποι δυνήσονται θαυμάζειν.
οἱ ἄνδρες δυνήσονται θαυμάζειν.
   • ἄνθρωπος car refer to men or women, while ἀνήρ can only refer to men.

5. The woman became happy.
ἡ γυνὴ ἐγένετο εὐδαίμων.
   • Remember that the masculine and feminine endings for 3rd declension adjectives like εὐδαίμων are the same.

6. I did not make justice.

οὐκ εἰργασάμην τὴν δικαιοσύνην.

δικαιοσύνην οὐκ εἰργασάμην.

Chapter 16 〜

1. ἐγὼ μόνος ἐσώθην ὑπὸ τῆς ἐμῆς εὐσεβείας. (Chariton, *Chaereas and Callirhoë*)

I alone was saved by my reverence.

Only I was saved by my piety.

2. τόλμα ἀλόγιστος ἀνδρεία φιλέταιρος ἐνομίσθη. (Thucydides, *History of the Peloponnesian War*)

Foolish boldness was considered loyal courage.

Thoughtless boldness was thought to be loyal bravery.

3. καὶ γὰρ ὁ υἱὸς τοῦ ἀνθρώπου οὐκ ἦλθεν διακονηθῆναι ἀλλὰ διακονῆσαι. (Mark 10:45)

For indeed the son of man did not come to be served, but to serve.

4. ὃ θέλεις φέρε κἀγὼ αὐτὸ ἀγαθὸν ποιήσω. (Epictetus, *Discourses*)

Bring what you wish and I will make it good.

- For Stoics, external events were neither good nor bad; good and bad were dependent upon one's reactions to those external events.

5. χρυσὸς ἀνοίγει πάντα κἀΐδου πύλας. (Menander, *Fragments*)

Gold opens all things, even the gates of Hades.

6. λογίζομαι γὰρ ὅτι οὐκ ἄξια τὰ παθήματα τοῦ νῦν καιροῦ πρὸς τὴν μέλλουσαν δόξαν ἀποκαλυφθῆναι εἰς ἡμᾶς. (Romans 8:18)

For I think that the sufferings of the present age are not worthy to be compared to the coming glory to be revealed to us.

For I consider that the sufferings of the present are not worthy compared to the glory about to be revealed to us.

7. ὁ δὲ ἀγαπῶν με ἀγαπηθήσεται ὑπὸ τοῦ πατρός μου, κἀγὼ ἀγαπήσω αὐτὸν καὶ ἐμφανίσω αὐτῷ ἐμαυτόν. (John 14:21)
And the one loving me will be loved by my Father, and I will love him, and I will reveal myself to him.

- You will learn more about participles in chapter 19. Greek loves participles, where English prefers relative clauses. It is for this reason that you will often see participles translated as relative clauses, such as "the one who loves me" in place of "the one loving me." I would suggest not turning participial phrases into relative clauses until you are firmly in command of the grammar of these two constructions.

8. καὶ ἐπλήσθη πνεύματος ἁγίου ἡ Ἐλισάβετ. (Luke 1:41)
And Elizabeth was filled with the Holy Spirit.

9. πᾶς ὁ ὑψῶν ἑαυτὸν ταπεινωθήσεται καὶ ὁ ταπεινῶν ἑαυτὸν ὑψωθήσεται. (Matthew 23:12)
Everyone exalting himself will be humbled, and everyone humbling himself will be exalted.

Everyone raising himself up will be brought low, and everyone lowering himself will be raised up.

10. μακάριοι οἱ πτωχοὶ τῷ πνεύματι, ὅτι αὐτῶν ἐστιν ἡ βασιλεία τῶν οὐρανῶν.
Fortunate are the poor in spirit, because the kingdom of heaven is theirs.
Blessed are the poor in spirit, because the kingdom of heaven is theirs.
Happy are the beggarly in spirit, since of them is the kingdom of heaven.

- As was explained in the notes to sentence 7, many translators will use relative clauses in the beatitudes, "Blessed are those who," etc. This is not wrong, but I would use literal translations until you have a command of both constructions.

- It is not wrong to translate μακάριοι as "blessed" in the beatitudes, but it does obscure the shocking pronouncements in the beatitudes.

- Technically τῶν οὐρανῶν is plural, so "kingdom of the heavens," but the plural and singular are used interchangeably, so keeping "kingdom of heaven" in your translation is fine.

μακάριοι οἱ πενθοῦντες, ὅτι αὐτοὶ παρακληθήσονται.
Fortunate are the mourners, because they will be comforted.

μακάριοι οἱ πραεῖς, ὅτι αὐτοὶ κληρονομήσουσι τὴν γῆν.
Fortunate are the gentle, because they will inherit the earth.
Fortunate are the meek, because they will inherit the land.

μακάριοι οἱ πεινῶντες καὶ διψῶντες τὴν δικαιοσύνην, ὅτι αὐτοὶ χορτασθήσονται.
Fortunate are those hungering and thirsting for righteousness, because they will be satisfied.
Happy are those hungering and thirsting for righteousness, because they will be filled.

μακάριοι οἱ ἐλεήμονες, ὅτι αὐτοὶ ἐλεηθήσονται.
Fortunate are those pitying, because they will be pitied.
Happy are those showing mercy, because they will be shown mercy.

μακάριοι οἱ καθαροὶ τῇ καρδίᾳ, ὅτι αὐτοὶ τὸν θεὸν ὄψονται.
Fortunate are the pure in heart, because they will see God.

μακάριοι οἱ εἰρηνοποιοί, ὅτι αὐτοὶ υἱοὶ θεοῦ κληθήσονται.
Fortunate are the peace-makers, because they will be called sons of God.

μακάριοι οἱ δεδιωγμένοι ἕνεκεν δικαιοσύνης, ὅτι αὐτῶν ἐστιν ἡ βασιλεία τῶν οὐρανῶν.
Fortunate are those persecuted for the sake of righteousness, because the kingdom of heaven is theirs.

(Matthew 5:3–10)

Supplementary Exercises

Change the following aorist middle forms into aorist passive forms.

Aorist Middle Indicative	Aorist Passive Indicative	Aorist Middle Indicative	Aorist Passive Indicative
ἐλυσάμεθα	ἐλύθημεν	ἐλύσατο	ἐλύθη
ἐλύσω	ἐλύθης	ἐλύσαντο	ἐλύθησαν
ἐλυσάμην	ἐλύθην	ἐλύσασθε	ἐλύθητε

Change the following future middle forms into future passive forms.

Future Middle Indicative	Future Passive Indicative	Future Middle Indicative	Future Passive Indicative
λύσομαι	λυθήσομαι	λυσόμεθα	λυθησόμεθα
λύσει	λυθήσῃ/σει	λύσεσθε	λυθήσεσθε
λύσονται	λυθήσονται	λύσεται	λυθήσεται

Write out the individual words constituting each of the following examples of crasis.

1. κἀγώ   καὶ ἐγώ
2. ταὐτά   τὰ αὐτά
3. κἀμοί   καὶ ἐμοί

Translate the following sentences into Greek.

¶ ἀνήρ, ανδρός, ὁ = man; husband

1. The merciful will be called pure.

οἱ ἐλεήμονες κληθήσονται καθαροί.

2. The gentle man was comforted.

ὁ πραῢς ἀνὴρ παρεκλήθη.

3. Merciful things were done by the pure alone.

τὰ ἐλεήμονα ἐποιήθησαν ὑπὸ τῶν καθαρῶν μόνων.

4. Our bravery was not seen.

ἡ ἀνδρεία ἡμῶν οὐκ ὤφθη.

5. Serve (plural) the gentle.

διακονεῖτε (present imperative) τοὺς πραεῖς.

διακονήσατε (aorist imperative) τοὺς πραεῖς.

6. My bravery will be summoned.

ἡ ἀνδρεία ἐμοῦ παρακληθήσεται.

ἡ ἐμὴ ἀνδρεία παρακληθήσεται.

Chapter 17 ～

1. ἔγνων ὡς θεὸς ἦσθα. (*Homeric Hymn to Aphrodite*)
I knew that you were a god.

2. ἡ μὲν ἔβη πρὸς δῶμα Διὸς θυγάτηρ Ἀφροδίτη. (Homer, *Iliad*)
Aphrodite the daughter of Zeus went towards home.
She went home, Aphrodite the daughter of Zeus.
   - The definite article will sometimes be used where we would use a 3rd person personal pronoun.

3. Οἰδίπους εἰμί, ὃς τὰ κλείν᾽ αἰνίγματ᾽ ἔγνων καὶ μέγιστος ἦν ἀνήρ. (Euripides, *Phoenician Women*)
I am Oedipus, who knew the famous riddle and was the greatest man.
I am Oedipus, who knew the famous riddles and was the greatest man.
   - αἰνίγματα is here a poetic plural, so the singular is an acceptable translation.

4. ἐν τῷ κόσμῳ ἦν, καὶ ὁ κόσμος δι᾽ αὐτοῦ ἐγένετο, καὶ ὁ κόσμος αὐτὸν οὐκ ἔγνω. (John 1:10)
He was in the world, and the world came to be through him, but the world did not know him.
   - Sometimes καὶ has the sense of "but" rather than "and."

5. φονέα σέ φημι τἀνδρὸς ὃν ζητεῖς κυρεῖν. (Sophocles, *Oedipus Tyrannus*)
I say that you are the murderer of the man whom you are seeking to find.

- While English necessitates the placement of the verb before the indirect statement, notice how the emphatic word is placed at the beginning of the line.

6. εἰ μέν σοι δοκῶ ἐγὼ καλῶς λέγειν, φάθι, εἰ δὲ μή, ἔλεγχε καὶ μὴ ἐπίτρεπε.
(Socrates, in Plato, *Gorgias*)
If I seem to you to speak beautifully, speak, and if not, question me and do not give up.
If I seem to you to speak well, say so, but if not, question me and do not yield.

- You must supply the understood word "me."

7. αὐτόματοι δ᾽ ἀγαθοὶ δειλῶν ἐπὶ δαῖτας ἴασιν. (Traditional Proverb)
Of their own accord the good go to the feasts of the lowborn.
On their own the good go to the feats of the cowardly.

8. ἔφη αὐτῷ ὁ Ἰησοῦς, "Εἰ θέλεις τέλειος εἶναι, ὕπαγε πώλησόν σου τὰ ὑπάρχοντα καὶ δὸς τοῖς πτωχοῖς, καὶ ἕξεις θησαυρὸν ἐν οὐρανοῖς."
(Matthew 19:21)
Jesus said to him, "If you want to be perfect, go, sell your possessions and give them to the poor, and you will have treasure in heaven.

- You must supply the understood word "them".

9. τοὺς βουλομένους ἀθανάτους εἶναι ἔφη δεῖν εὐσεβῶς καὶ δικαίως ζῆν.
(Antisthenes, in Diogenes Laertius, *Lives of Eminent Philosophers*)
He said that it is necessary that those wishing to be immortal live reverently and justly.
Antisthenes said that it was necessary for those wishing to be immortal to live piously and justly.

10. ἄνδρα μοι ἔννεπε, Μοῦσα, πολύτροπον, ὃς μάλα πολλὰ
πλάγχθη, ἐπεὶ Τροίης ἱερὸν πτολίεθρον ἔπερσε·
πολλῶν δ᾽ ἀνθρώπων ἴδεν ἄστεα καὶ νόον ἔγνω. (Homer, *Odyssey*)
Muse, tell me of the many-turning man, who was turned aside in many ways after he sacked the holy citadel of Troy. He saw the cities of many peoples and knew their mind.

- As is often the case in poetry, there are many possible translations. This is a very unartful and literal translation.
- Notice the placement of ἄνδρα at the beginning of the line. It is the accusative direct object of the imperative ἔννεπε, but in English it sounds odd unless we add an "of" before "man."

Supplementary Exercises

Translate the following sentences into Greek.

❡ ἀνήρ, ανδρός, ὁ = man; husband | γυνή, γυναικός, ἡ = woman; wife | εὐδαίμων, –ον (adj.) = fortunate, happy

1. Zeus knew the cowardly man.
Ζεὺς ἔγνω τὸν δειλὸν ἄνδρα.
τὸν δειλὸν ἄνδρα Ζεὺς ἔγνω.

2. Zeus will go to the famous men.
Ζεὺς εἶσι πρὸς τοὺς κλεινοὺς ἄνδρας.
πρὸς τοὺς κλεινοὺς ἄνδρας Ζεὺς εἶσιν.

3. The husband was questioned by the wife.
ὁ ἀνὴρ ἠλέγχθη (aorist) ὑπὸ τῆς γυναικός.
ὁ ἀνὴρ ἠλέγχετο (imperfect) ὑπὸ τῆς γυναικός.
   - The imperfect would be used if the author viewed the questioning as an event taking place over time.

4. We denied that the riddle was famous.
οὐκ ἔφαμεν (imperfect) τὸ αἴνιγμα εἶναι κλεινόν.
ἐφήσαμεν (aorist) τὸ αἴνιγμα οὐκ εἶναι κλεινόν.
   - The use of the aorist is very rare. You will see the imperfect used far more often.

Chapter 18 ～

1. ἡ βασιλεία ἡ ἐμὴ οὐκ ἔστιν ἐκ τοῦ κόσμου τούτου. (John 18:36)
My kingdom is not of this world.

2. τοῦτο μόνον θέλω μαθεῖν ἀφ᾿ ὑμῶν, ἐξ ἔργων νόμου τὸ πνεῦμα ἐλάβετε ἢ
ἐξ ἀκοῆς πίστεως; (Gal 3:2)
I wish to learn only this from you, did you receive the Spirit from works
of the law or from hearing the faith?
This alone I want to learn from you, did you receive the Spirit by works
of the law or by the hearing of faith?

- Greek often uses the preposition ἐκ to express the source, and hence
the cause of something. "From" usually works as a translation, but
"by" or other words denoting agency sometimes sound better.

3. οὗτος ἁμαρτωλοὺς προσδέχεται καὶ συνεσθίει αὐτοῖς. (Luke 15:2)
This man receives sinners and eats with them.
He receives sinners and eats with them.

- Because Greek (especially Classical Greek) prefers not to use
αὐτός-ή-όν as a 3rd person pronoun in the nominative, it is common
to see the demonstrative perform this function. In such cases a
"he/she/it" translation is preferable to "this."

4. ἀδιαλείπτως προσεύχεσθε, ἐν παντὶ εὐχαριστεῖτε· τοῦτο γὰρ θέλημα θεοῦ
ἐν Χριστῷ Ἰησοῦ εἰς ὑμᾶς. (1 Thess 5:17–18)
Pray continuously, give thanks in everything. For this is the will of God
in Christ Jesus for you.

Pray without ceasing, give thanks in everything. For this is the will of God for you in Christ Jesus.

5. σοφοὶ δὲ ἐνομίζοντο οἵδε· Θαλῆς, Σόλων, Περίανδρος, Κλεόβουλος, Χείλων, Βίας, Πιττακός. (Diogenes Laertius, *Lives of Eminent Philosophers*)
These were considered the wise men: Thales, Solon, Periander, Cleobolus, Cheilon, Bias, Pittacus.
The following were considered sages: Thales, Solon, Periander, Cleobolus, Cheilon, Bias, Pittacus.

6. ἦν Λακεδαιμόνιος Χείλων σοφός, ὃς τάδ᾽ ἔλεξε· μηδὲν ἄγαν· καιρῷ πάντα πρόσεστι καλά. (Diogenes Laertius, *Lives of Eminent Philosophers*)
The Lacedemonian Cheilon was a sage, who said the following: Nothing too much. Everything beautiful belongs to kairos.
The Spartan Cheilon was a sage who said the following: Nothing in excess, all things are beautiful at the proper time.

- Translating καιρός literally can be difficult. The goal is to eventually not need to find an English equivalent, but to just think "καιρός." Of course it will take some time before this happens, but if you find yourself knowing what a Greek word means and being frustrated having to put it into English, that is a good sign.

7. τὸ πνεῦμα τὸ ἅγιον ὃ πέμψει ὁ πατὴρ ἐν τῷ ὀνόματί μου, ἐκεῖνος ὑμᾶς διδάξει πάντα καὶ ὑπομνήσει ὑμᾶς πάντα ἃ εἶπον ὑμῖν ἐγώ. (John 14:26)
The Holy Spirit which my father will send in my name, that one will teach you everything and remind you everything which I said to you.
The Holy Spirit which my Father will send in my name, He will teach you everything and remind you everything which I said to you.

8. καὶ ἔλεγεν, "Ἀββα ὁ πατήρ, πάντα δυνατά σοι· παρένεγκε τὸ ποτήριον τοῦτο ἀπ᾽ ἐμοῦ· ἀλλ᾽ οὐ τί ἐγὼ θέλω ἀλλὰ τί σύ." (Mark 14:36)
And he said, Abba, "Father," all things are possible for you. Remove this cup from me. But not what I will but what you will.

- This sentence is difficult to translate because "Father, Father" sounds odd.

- The words ὁ πατήρ are not the words of Jesus, but of Mark telling the reader what Ἀββα means.

9. οὔτε γὰρ ὁ ἐλλείπων τῇ ὀργῇ οὔτε ὁ ὑπερβάλλων ἐπαινετός ἐστιν, ἀλλ᾽ ὁ μέσως ἔχων πρὸς ταῦτα, οὗτος πραΰς. (Aristotle, *Magna Moralia*)

For neither the one lacking in anger nor the one in excess in anger is praiseworthy, but the one being moderate with respect to these things, this one is gentle.

For praiseworthy is neither the one lacking nor in excess with respect to anger, but the one being moderate with respect to these, he is meek.

10. Socrates: ὅς ἀγαθὸς ῥαψῳδός ἐστιν, οὗτος καὶ ἀγαθὸς στρατηγός ἐστιν;

Ion: μάλιστα, ὦ Σώκρατες.

Socrates: οὐκοῦν καὶ ὅς ἀγαθὸς στρατηγός ἐστιν, ἀγαθὸς καὶ ῥαψῳδός ἐστιν;

Ion: οὐκ αὖ μοι δοκεῖ τοῦτο.

Socrates: ἀλλ᾽ ἐκεῖνο δοκεῖ σοι, ὅς ἀγαθὸς ῥαψῳδός, καὶ στρατηγὸς ἀγαθὸς εἶναι;

Ion: πάνυ γε.

(Plato, *Ion*)

Socrates: He who is a good rhapsode, is he also a good general?

Ion: Absolutely, oh Socrates.

Socrates: Surely then he who is a good general is also a good rhapsode?

Ion: This, on the other hand, does not seem right to me.

Socrates: But that seems right to you, that he who is a good rhapsode is also a good general?

Ion: No doubt.

Supplementary Exercises

Add the corresponding form of each demonstrative (οὗτος, ἐκεῖνος, ὅδε) to the following nouns.

¶ γυνή, γυναικός, ἡ = woman; wife | παιδίον, –ου, τό = child

οὗτος ἐκεῖνος   ὅδε

ὁ ἁμαρτωλός	οὗτος	ἐκεῖνος	ὅδε
τὰ παιδία	ταῦτα	ἐκεῖνα	τάδε
τῇ γυναικί	ταύτῃ	ἐκείνῃ	τῇδε
τοὺς στρατηγούς	τούτους	ἐκείνους	τούσδε
τῶν στρατηγῶν	τούτων	ἐκείνων	τῶνδε

Translate the following sentences into Greek.

γιγνώσκω, γνώσομαι, ἔγνων, —, —, ἐγνώσθην = to know | ἐλέγχω, ἐλέγξω, ἤλεγξα = to cross-examine, question | πράττω (Koine πράσσω), πράξω, ἔπραξα, πέπραγμα or (πέπραχα), πέπραγμαι, ἐπράχθην = to do

1. This sinner prays; that sinner does not pray.
οὗτος ὁ ἁμαρτωλὸς προσεύχεται, ἐκεῖνος ὁ ἁμαρτωλὸς οὐκ προσεύχεται.
ὁ μὲν ἁμαρτωλὸς οὗτος προσεύχεται, ἐκεῖνος δὲ οὐ.

2. Those generals questioned the wise men.
οἱ στρατηγοὶ ἐκεῖνοι ἤλεγξαν τοὺς σοφοὺς ἄνδρας.
ἐκεῖνοι οἱ στρατηγοὶ ἤλεγξαν τοὺς σοφοὺς ἄνδρας.

3. I know that this general is wise.
γιγνώσκω ὅτι οὗτος ὁ στρατηγός ἐστι σοφός.

4. I know this: the wise man does wise things.
γιγνώσκω τόδε· ὁ σοφὸς πράττει τὰ σοφά.
γιγνώσκω τόδε· ὁ σοφὸς πράσσει τὰ σοφά.

5. The wise men will know that opportunity.
οἱ σοφοὶ γνώσονται ἐκεῖνον τὸν καιρόν.

6. Let the wise man pray.
προσευξάσθω (aorist imperative) ὁ σοφός.
προσευχέσθω (present imperative) ὁ σοφός

7. These things will be known by those people.

τὰ ταῦτα γνωσθήσεται ὑπ᾽ ἐκείνων τῶν ἀνθρώπων.

- Remember that neuter plural subjects take singular verbs.

Chapter 19 ∾

1. πάντα δυνατὰ τῷ πιστεύοντι. (Mark 9:23)
All things are possible for the one trusting.
All things are possible for the believer.
Everything is possible for the one having faith.

2. φεῦγ' ἡδονὴν φέρουσαν ὑστέρην βλάβην. (Alexis, *Fragments*)
Flee pleasure bearing later harm.
Flee the pleasure which brings later harm.

3. οὐ δεῖ ὥσπερ καθεύδοντας ποιεῖν καὶ λέγειν. (Heraclitus, *Fragments*)
It is necessary to not do and speak as ones asleep.
It is necessary that we not act and speak as though asleep.

4. ὁ μὴ δαρεὶς ἄνθρωπος οὐ παιδεύεται. (Menander, *Fragments*)
The person not thrashed is not educated.

5. τὰ γὰρ βλεπόμενα πρόσκαιρα, τὰ δὲ μὴ βλεπόμενα αἰώνια. (2 Cor 4:18)
For the things seen are temporary, but the things not seen are eternal.
   • The verb "are" must be supplied in your translation.

6. ἀμὴν ἀμὴν λέγω ὑμῖν, ὁ πιστεύων ἔχει ζωὴν αἰώνιον. (John 6:47)
Amen, amen I say to you, the one trusting has eternal life.
Truly, truly I say to you, the one having faith has eternal life.

7. Ἀμὴν ἀμὴν λέγω ὑμῖν ὅτι πᾶς ὁ ποιῶν τὴν ἁμαρτίαν δοῦλός ἐστιν τῆς ἁμαρτίας. (John 8:34)

Amen, amen, I say to you that everyone doing sin is a slave of sin.

Verily, verily, I say to you that everyone doing sin is a slave of sin.

- Some prefer to leave amen untranslated, while others prefer to translate it by words such as "truly" and "verily."

8. καὶ ἀνεφώνησεν κραυγῇ μεγάλῃ καὶ εἶπεν, "Εὐλογημένη σὺ ἐν γυναιξίν, καὶ εὐλογημένος ὁ καρπὸς τῆς κοιλίας σου." (Luke 1:42)

And she shouted with a great shout and said "Blessed are you among women, and blessed is the fruit of your womb."

And she exclaimed with a great cry and said "You are blessed among women, and blessed is the fruit of your womb."

9. ἀνὴρ δίκαιός ἐστιν οὐχ ὁ μὴ ἀδικῶν. (Philemon, *Fragments*)

One not being unjust is not simply a just man.

A just man is not simply one not being unjust.

Merely avoiding injustice does not make one just.

- The last translation is very liberal, yet it captures the meaning of the sentence.

10.   δέομαι ποιητοῦ δεξιοῦ. οἱ μὲν γὰρ οὐκέτ᾽ εἰσίν, οἱ δ᾽ ὄντες κακοί. (Aristophanes, *Frogs*)

I need a skilled poet. For they no longer exist, and the ones that exist are bad.

Supplementary Exercises

Identify the gender, number, case, tense, and voice of the following participles.

The words followed by empty spaces are words that can be multiple separate cases. Write all forms.

	Gender	Number	Case	Tense	Voice
ὤν	masculine	singular	nominative	present	active
ὄν	neuter	singular	nominative	present	active
	neuter	singular	accusative	present	active
οὔσης	feminine	singular	genitive	present	active
ὄντων	m/f/n	plural	genitive	present	active
λύοντα	masculine	singular	accusative	present	active
	neuter	plural	nominative	present	active
	neuter	plural	accusative	present	active
λύοντας	masculine	plural	accusative	present	active
λυομένην	feminine	singular	accusative	present	middle/passive
λύσουσαι	feminine	plural	nominative	future	active
λυσόμενοι	masculine	plural	nominative	future	middle
λύσαντος	masculine/neuter	singular	genitive	aorist	active
λυσομένῳ	masculine	singular	dative	future	middle
	neuter	singular	dative	future	middle
λυθησομένους	masculine	plural	accusative	future	passive
λυθείς	masculine	singular	nominative	aorist	passive
λυθεῖσιν	masculine	plural	dative	aorist	passive
	neuter	plural	dative	aorist	passive

Translate the following sentences into Greek.

¶ γιγνώσκω, γνώσομαι, ἔγνων, —, —, ἐγνώσθην = to know | εἰμί = to be | λέγω = to speak | πράττω (Koine πράσσω) = to do

1. A harm done is eternal.

ἡ πραχθεῖσα (aorist participle) βλάβη ἐστὶν αἰώνιος.

ἡ πραττομένη (present participle) βλάβη ἐστὶν αἰώνιος.

- αἰώνιος, -ον does not have separate feminine forms, hence αἰώνιος, not αἰώνια, a form which does not exist.

2. The poets speaking eternal things are not servile.

οἱ λέγοντες τὰ αἰώνια ποιηταὶ οὐκ εἰσὶ δοῦλοι.

- ποιηταὶ is a masculine first declension noun, hence οἱ and δοῦλοι.

3. Let the slaves flee.

φυγόντων οἱ δοῦλοι.

4. We will need the poets.

δεησόμεθα τοὺς ποιητάς.

δεησόμεθα τῶν ποιητῶν.

5. We do not need a poet speaking servile things.

οὐ δεόμεθα τοῦ λεγομένου τὰ δοῦλα ποιητοῦ.

6. The harms of the poets were known.

αἱ βλάβαι τῶν ποιητῶν ἐγνώσθησαν.

7. Eternal is the mistake of the poet.

αἰώνιός ἐστιν ἡ ἁμαρτία τοῦ ποιητοῦ.

Chapter 20 〜

1. ὁ γραμμάτων ἄπειρος οὐ βλέπει βλέπων. (Menander, *Fragments*)
The one without experience of letters seeing, does not see.
The one ignorant of letters does not see, even though he sees.
Although he sees, the man ignorant of letters does not see.

2. ἀδικεῖ Σωκράτης, οὓς μὲν ἡ πόλις νομίζει θεοὺς οὐ νομίζων, ἕτερα δὲ καινὰ δαιμόνια εἰσηγούμενος. (Xenophon, *Memorabilia*)
Socrates is unjust, not thinking those whom the city thinks are gods are gods, but introducing other new deities.
Socrates is unjust, since he does not believe in those gods in whom the city believes, but introduces other new spirits.
  • As I explain in the book, I am generally a proponent of translating circumstantial participles literally. I will, however, include translations in this chapter that use the standard adverbial phrases.

3. ὡς τὸν αὐτὸν οἶνον πίνοντες οἱ μὲν παροινοῦσιν οἱ δὲ πραΰνονται, οὕτω καὶ πλοῦτον. (Ariston, in Stobaeus, *Anthology*)
Just as, drinking the same wine, some become calm and some behave ill, so too concerning money.
Just as, when they drink the same wine, some become calm while others are bad drunks, the same applies to money.
Just as, even though they drink the same wine, some become calm while others are bad drunks, so too with money.

4.   βλάπτει τὸν ἄνδρα θυμὸς εἰς ὀργὴν πεσών. (Menander, *Fragments*)
The spirit, falling into anger, harms a man.
When the spirit falls into anger, it harms a man.
The spirit harms a man when it falls into anger.

5.   ἡγεῖται δὲ πάντα ταῦτα τὰ κτήματα οὐδενὸς ἄξια καὶ ἡμᾶς οὐδὲν εἶναι—
λέγω ὑμῖν—εἰρωνευόμενος δὲ καὶ παίζων πάντα τὸν βίον πρὸς τοὺς
ἀνθρώπους διατελεῖ. (Plato, *Symposium*)
And he thinks all these things and possessions are worthy of nothing...and
that we are nothing, I tell you, he spends all his life feigning ignorance and
jesting with people.
And he considers all these things and possessions to be worthy of nothing,
and thinks we are nothing, I tell you, but he lives all his life feigning ignorance and jesting with men.

6.   ὁ δὲ θεὸς πλούσιος ὢν ἐν ἐλέει, διὰ τὴν πολλὴν ἀγάπην αὐτοῦ ἣν ἠγάπησεν
ἡμᾶς, καὶ ὄντας ἡμᾶς νεκροὺς τοῖς παραπτώμασιν συνεζωοποίησεν τῷ
Χριστῷ. (Eph 2:4–5)
But God, being rich in mercy, on account of the great love with which he
loved us, brought us, being dead, to life with Christ.
But God, since he is rich in mercy, because of the great love by which he
loved us, brought us to life in Christ, although we were dead.

7. καὶ ἐταράχθη Ζαχαρίας ἰδών, καὶ φόβος ἐπέπεσεν ἐπ᾽ αὐτόν. εἶπεν δὲ πρὸς
αὐτὸν ὁ ἄγγελος, "Μὴ φοβοῦ, Ζαχαρία, διότι εἰσηκούσθη ἡ δέησίς σου, καὶ ἡ
γυνή σου Ἐλισάβετ γεννήσει υἱόν σοι, καὶ καλέσεις τὸ ὄνομα αὐτοῦ Ἰωάννην."
(Luke 1:12–13)
And Zacharias, seeing was shaken, and fear fell upon him. And the messenger said to him, "Do not fear, Zacharias, for your prayer was heard, and
your wife Elizabeth will bear a son to you, and you will call his name John.
And when he saw the angel, Zacharias was shaken, and fear fell upon him.
And the angel said to him, "Do not be afraid, Zacharias, for your prayer
has been heard, and your wife Elizabeth will bear a son to you, and you
will name him John."

- The Romans transliterated the Greek word ἄγγελος as angelus, from which we get our English word angel. Both "messenger" and "angel" work in scripture, but obviously "messenger" is the best translation in Classical Greek.

8 ἄνθρωπον ὄντα δεῖ φρονεῖν τἀνθρώπινα. (Menander, *Fragments*)
Being human, it is necessary to think human things.
Since you are human, it is necessary to think human things.
It is necessary for you, since you are human, to think human things.

9. ὃς ἐν μορφῇ θεοῦ ὑπάρχων οὐχ ἁρπαγμὸν ἡγήσατο τὸ εἶναι ἴσα θεῷ, ἀλλὰ ἑαυτὸν ἐκένωσεν μορφὴν δούλου λαβών. (Phil 2:6–7)
Who, being in the form of God, did not think being like God was something to be seized, but he emptied himself, taking the form of a servant.
Who, although he was in the form of God, did not think equality with God was something to be grasped, but rather, he emptied himself when he took the form of a slave.

- While the sense of ὑπάρχων seems to be concessive, "although," if one reads the whole passage, the participle could also be causal "since," as that is how Paul views God as behaving. This is one of the benefits to translating the participles literally, here "being."

10. ἀκούσας δέ τις τῶν συνανακειμένων ταῦτα εἶπεν αὐτῷ, Μακάριος ὅστις φάγεται ἄρτον ἐν τῇ βασιλείᾳ τοῦ θεοῦ. (Luke 14:15)
And one of those reclining with him, hearing these things, said to him, "Fortunate is he who eats bread in the kingdom of God."
And one of the guests, when he heard these things, said to him, "Blessed is he who eats bread in the kingdom of God."

Supplementary Exercises

Translate the following sentences into Greek. Next, state whether the sentence contains an attributive participle, a circumstantial participle, or both.
¶ ἄνθρωπος, –ου, ὁ = human being, person | κακός, –ή, –όν (adj.) = bad, base, evil | φεύγω, φεύξομαι, ἔφυγον, —, —, — = to flee

1. Having harmed the evil person, the angel fled.

βλάψας τὸν κακὸν ἄνθρωπον ὁ ἄγγελος ἔφυγεν.

ὁ ἄγγελος ἔφυγε βλάψας τὸν κακὸν ἄνθρωπον.

Circumstantial Participle

2. I fled the angel harming the evil person.

ἔφυγον τὸν βλάπτοντα τὸν κακὸν ἄνθρωπον ἄγγελον.

ἔφυγον τὸν ἄγγελον τὸν βλάπτοντα τὸν κακὸν ἄνθρωπον.

Attributive Participle

- Notice how important the correct identification of the participle is to the correct understanding of the sentence. If we used a circumstantial participle instead of an attributive participle, βλάπτων τὸν κακὸν ἄνθρωπον ἔφυγον τὸν ἄγγελον, we would get "Having harmed the evil person, I fled the angel," or "After I harmed the evil person, I fled the angel."
- Remember that both the above sentences contain an attributive participle, which is signified by placing a definite article right before the participle. You will see both (1) article + participle + noun and (2) article + noun + article + participle. Since the participle is a verbal adjective, the same rules of attributive position apply.

3. Being disturbed, the dead will harm us.

ταρασσόμενοι οἱ νεκροὶ βλάψουσιν ἡμᾶς.

Circumstantial Participle

4. The disturbed dead will harm us.

οἱ ταρασσόμενοι νεκροὶ βλάψουσιν ἡμᾶς.

Attributive Participle

5. Let them not flee, having harmed the dead.

βλάψαντες τοὺς νεκροὺς οὐ φυγόντων (aorist imperative).

οὐ φυγόντων βλάψαντες τοὺς νεκρούς.

Circumstantial Participle

6. Since mercy is not new, it is dead.

ὁ ἔλεος οὐκ ὤν καινός ἐστι νεκρός.

οὐκ ὤν καινὸς ὁ ἔλεός ἐστι νεκρός.

Circumstantial Participle

7. When mercy is not new, it is dead.

ὁ ἔλεος οὐκ ὤν καινός ἐστι νεκρός.

οὐκ ὤν καινὸς ὁ ἔλεός ἐστι νεκρός.

Circumstantial Participle

- Notice that the Greek for 6 and 7 is the same.

8. Although the angel was harmed, he (the angel) is not dead.

βλαβείς (aorist participle) ὁ ἄγγελος οὐκ ἔστι νεκρός.

Circumstantial Participle

Chapter 21 ～

1. εἰ δὲ τυγχάνεις κακὸς ὤν, ἡ κακία σε βλάπτει καὶ οὐχ ἡ φυγή. (Musonius, in Stobaeus, *Anthology*)

If you happen to be bad, the badness harms you and not the exile.

If you happen to be evil, evil harms you, not exile.

2. ὁ σοφιστὴς τυγχάνει ὢν ἔμπορος ἢ κάπηλος τῶν ἀγωγίμων ὑφ᾽ ὧν ψυχὴ τρέφεται; (Plato, *Protagoras*)

Does the sophist happen to be a merchant or huckster of provisions by which the soul is nourished?

Does the sophist happen to be a merchant or dealer of provisions which nourish the soul?

- The second translation is not wrong, but for beginning students I recommend keeping active constructions active and passive constructions passive.

3. οὐδεὶς ποιῶν πονηρὰ λανθάνει θεόν. (Menander, *Fragments*)

No one doing wicked things escapes the notice of god.

No one doing evil does so without a god's notice.

4. εἶδεν ὁ Ἰησοῦς τὸν Ναθαναὴλ ἐρχόμενον πρὸς αὐτὸν καὶ λέγει περὶ αὐτοῦ, "Ἴδε ἀληθῶς Ἰσραηλίτης ἐν ᾧ δόλος οὐκ ἔστιν." (John 1:47)

Jesus saw Nathaniel coming towards him and said about him, "Behold, truly an Israelite in whom there is no treachery."

Jesus saw Nathaniel coming towards him and said of him, "Behold, a true Israelite in whom there is no deceit."

- Technically ἀληθῶς is an adverb, but, as we have seen, Greek often uses an adverb where English would use an adjective.

5. αὐτοὶ δ᾽ ἁμαρτάνοντες οὐ γιγνώσκομεν. (Euripides, *Fragments*)
That we ourselves are sinning, we do not know.
We do not know that we ourselves are sinners.
- This one is tricky to translate into English. αὐτοὶ is an intensive, so we would normally translate it as "sinners themselves," or "the very ones sinning." Once we get to the first person verb, however, it is clear that we are the subject. It is a fragment, so we don't know the context, but perhaps that was the intention of the line.

6. λέγουσι ὅτι τῆς μητρὸς ἀναγκαζούσης αὐτὸν γῆμαι ἔλεγεν, "οὐδέπω καιρός." εἶτα, ἐπειδὴ παρήβησεν, ἔλεγεν, "οὐκέτι καιρός." (Thales, in Diogenes Laertius, *Lives of Eminent Philosophers*)
They say that, his mother compelling him to marry, he used to say, "It is not yet time." Then, when he was elderly, he used to say, "It is no longer time."
They say that, when his mother compelled him to marry, Thales said, "It is not yet time." Then, when he was past his prime, he said, "It is no longer time."
- Pay attention to the use of the imperfect ἔλεγεν rather than the aorist. The imperfect represents habitual or ongoing action in the past. One can hardly believe his mother would have only mentioned it once!

7. γενομένης δὲ ἡμέρας ἐξελθὼν ἐπορεύθη εἰς ἔρημον τόπον. (Luke 4:42)
Day coming to be, departing he went into a deserted place.
When it was day, he departed and went into the desert.
- Since genitive absolutes are just circumstantial participles whose subjects are different from the finite verb, the same rules of "when/since/although, etc." apply.

8. ἐμφόβων δὲ γενομένων αὐτῶν καὶ κλινουσῶν τὰ πρόσωπα εἰς τὴν γῆν εἶπαν πρὸς αὐτάς, "Τί ζητεῖτε τὸν ζῶντα μετὰ τῶν νεκρῶν;" (Luke 24:5)

Becoming afraid and bending their faces to the earth, to them the angels said, "Why do you seek the living one among the dead."

And when they became afraid and bowed their faces to the ground, the angels said to them, "Why do you seek one who lives among the dead."

- While it is not wrong, the traditional translation of "seek the living among the dead" obscures the fact that while the dead are plural, τὸν ζῶντα is singular. They know the women have come to search for one person.

- This sentence illustrates why a genitive absolute must be used instead of a circumstantial participle in the nominative. If a circumstantial participle were used, its subject would have to be the same as the subject of εἶπαν.

9. καὶ ὑστερήσαντος οἴνου λέγει ἡ μήτηρ τοῦ Ἰησοῦ πρὸς αὐτόν, "Οἶνον οὐκ ἔχουσιν." (John 2:3)

And the wine being empty, the mother of Jesus said to him, "They do not have wine."

When the wine was empty, the mother of Jesus said to him, "They have no wine."

10. ὁ βάρβαρος τῷ μεγάλῳ στόλῳ ἐπὶ τὴν Ἑλλάδα δουλωσόμενος ἦλθεν. (Thucydides, *History of the Peloponnesian War*)

The barbarian came with a great expedition to Greece to enslave it.

The barbarian came with a great expedition to enslave Greece.

- The future active participle is here being used to express purpose.

Supplementary Exercises

Translate the following sentences and identify whether each sentence contains an (1) attributive participle, a (2) circumstantial participle, or (3) a supplementary participle

❡ ἄνθρωπος, –ου, ὁ = human being, person | ἐπί (prep.) = on, upon (+ gen.), on, by, for (+ dat.), to, against (+ acc.) | ὑπό (prep.) = under, by (+ gen.) | ἐκεῖνος, ἐκείνη, ἐκεῖνο (demonstrative adj.) = that, the former

1. ὁ σοφιστὴς τρέφων τὸν δόλον, ἥμαρτεν.

The sophist, nourishing treachery, erred.

The sophist, since he nourished treachery, erred.

The sophist, by nourishing treachery, erred.

- It is best not to use "to sin" for ἁμαρτάνω in Classical Greek.
- Circumstantial Participle

2. παῦε τρέφων τὸν δόλον.

Cease nourishing treachery.

Stop rearing treachery.

- Supplementary Participle

3. ἔτυχον (1st person) πορεόμενος ἐπὶ ἐκεῖνον τόπον.

I happened to go to that place.

- Supplementary Participle

4. οὐκ ἀναγκάσομεν τοὺς ἀνθρώπους τοὺς ἀναγκασθέντας ὑπὸ τῶν σοφιστῶν.

We will not compel the men having been compelled by the sophists.

We will not compel the men who were compelled by the sophists.

- Attributive Participle

5. ἐκεῖνος σοφιστὴς λανθάνει Ἑλλάδα ἁμαρτάνων.

That sophist errs without the knowledge of Greece.

- Supplementary Participle

Translate the following sentences into Greek.

¶ ἀκούω = to hear | ἄνθρωπος, –ου, ὁ = human being, person | ἐκεῖνος, ἐκείνη, ἐκεῖνο (demonstrative adj.) = that; the former | ἀκούω = to hear

1. Stop (singular) compelling Greece to err.

παύου ἀναγκάζων Ἑλλάδα ἁμαρτάνειν.

2. The Sophists erred without the knowledge of Greece.

οἱ σοφισταὶ ἁμαρτάνοντες ἔλαθον Ἑλλάδα.

3. I did not come to compel the Sophists to cease.

οὐκ ἦλθον ἀναγκάσων τοὺς σοφιστὰς παύεσθαι.

οὐκ ἐπορευσάμην ἀναγκάσων τοὺς σοφιστὰς παύεσθαι.

4. When treachery ceases, Greece does not err.

δόλου παυομένου ἡ Ἑλλὰς οὐχ ἁμαρτάνουσιν.

5. I hear that the Sophists were coming to that place.

ἀκούω τοὺς σοφιστὰς πορευσαμένους ἐπὶ ἐκεῖνον τόπον.

ἀκούω τοὺς σοφιστὰς ἐλθόντας ἐπὶ ἐκεῖνον τόπον.

6. I heard that the Sophists would come to that place.

ἤκουσα τοὺς σοφιστὰς πορευσομένους ἐπὶ ἐκεῖνον τόπον.

ἤκουσα τοὺς σοφιστὰς ἐλευσομένους ἐπὶ ἐκεῖνον τόπον.

7. I heard that the Sophists had come to that place.

ἤκουσα τοὺς σοφιστὰς πορευσαμένους ἐπὶ ἐκεῖνον τόπον.

ἤκουσα τοὺς σοφιστὰς ἐλθόντας ἐπὶ ἐκεῖνον τόπον.

Chapter 22 ~

1. οὐδεὶς τὸ μέλλον ἀσφαλῶς ἐπίσταται. (Menander, *Fragments*)
No one knows the future with certainty.

2. ὁ Σωκράτης ἔλεγε καὶ ἓν μόνον ἀγαθὸν εἶναι, τὴν ἐπιστήμην, καὶ ἓν μόνον κακόν, τὴν ἀμαθίαν. (Diogenes Laertius, *Lives of Eminent Philosophers*)
Socrates used to say that there is only one good, knowledge, and only one evil, ignorance.
Socrates said that there was only one good, knowledge, and only one evil, ignorance.
- Remember that the ambiguity in the tense in these translations (is vs. was) is due to English, not Greek.
- The second translation of the imperfect is not wrong, but the imperfect shows that this was clearly something that he repeated.

3. ἐρωτηθεὶς τί ἐστι φίλος ὁ Ἀριστοτέλης ἔφη, "μία ψυχὴ δύο σώμασιν ἐνοικοῦσα." (Diogenes Laertius, *Lives of Eminent Philosophers*)
Having been asked what a friend is, Aristotle said "One soul inhabiting two bodies."

4. οὕτως γὰρ ἠγάπησεν ὁ θεὸς τὸν κόσμον, ὥστε τὸν υἱὸν τὸν μονογενῆ ἔδωκεν. (John 3:16)
For God so loved the world that he gave his only-begotten son.
For God loved the world so much that he gave his only-begotten son.

5. καὶ ἰδοὺ εἰσὶν ἔσχατοι οἳ ἔσονται πρῶτοι, καὶ εἰσὶν πρῶτοι οἳ ἔσονται ἔσχατοι. (Luke 13:30)

And behold, last are those who will be first, and they are first who will be last.

And behold, those who will be first are now last, and those who will be last are now first.

And behold, those are last who will be first, and those are first who will be last.

6. τέλος δὲ οἱ Στοϊκοί φασιν εἶναι τὸ εὐδαιμονεῖν, οὗ ἕνεκα πάντα πράττεται, αὐτὸ δὲ πράττεται οὐδενὸς ἕνεκα. (Stobaeus, *Anthology*)

And the Stoics say that happiness is the end for the sake of which all things are done, and it (happiness) is done for the sake of nothing.

- Remember that articular infinitives are impossible to translate literally "the to be happy," and are often best translated as nouns "happiness."

7. εἷς ἄρτος, ἓν σῶμα οἱ πολλοί ἐσμεν, οἱ γὰρ πάντες ἐκ τοῦ ἑνὸς ἄρτου μετέχομεν. (1 Cor 10:17)

One bread, one body, we many are. For we all partake of the one bread.

There is one bread, we who are many are one. For we all partake of the one bread.

8. καὶ λέγουσιν αὐτῷ οἱ μαθηταί, " Πόθεν ἡμῖν ἐν ἐρημίᾳ ἄρτοι τοσοῦτοι ὥστε χορτάσαι ὄχλον τοσοῦτον;" (Matthew 15:33)

The students say to him, "From where in the desert is there so much bread for us that could fill such a crowd?"

The disciples say to him, "Where in the desert is there so much bread for us that can fill such a crowd?"

9. καταλείψει ἄνθρωπος τὸν πατέρα καὶ τὴν μητέρα καὶ κολληθήσεται τῇ γυναικὶ αὐτοῦ, καὶ ἔσονται οἱ δύο εἰς σάρκα μίαν. ὥστε οὐκέτι εἰσὶν δύο ἀλλὰ σὰρξ μία. ὃ οὖν ὁ θεὸς συνέζευξεν ἄνθρωπος μὴ χωριζέτω. (Matthew 19:5–6)

A man will leave his father and mother and will be united to his wife, and the two will be one flesh, so that they are no longer two but one flesh. Therefore, what God joined together let man not separate.

A man will leave his father and mother and be joined to his wife, and the two will become one flesh, so that they are no longer two but one flesh. Therefore, what God had joined together, let no man divide.

10. καὶ ἰδοὺ σεισμὸς μέγας ἐγένετο ἐν τῇ θαλάσσῃ, ὥστε τὸ πλοῖον καλύπτεσθαι

ὑπὸ τῶν κυμάτων· αὐτὸς δὲ ἐκάθευδεν. (Matthew 8:24)

And behold, a great storm came to be on the sea, so that the boat was being covered by the waves. But he was sleeping.

And behold, there was a great storm on the sea, so that the boat was covered by the waves. But he was asleep.

- As is the case here, often in Koine a natural result clause will be used to express an actual result.

- καλύπτεσθαι is a present infinitive, so the aspect is imperfect "was being covered." As we have seen, it is also fine to use a simple past "covered."

Supplementary Exercises

Write the corresponding forms of ψυχή, ἄνθρωπος, and βιβλίον for each of the following numeric adjectives.

ψυχή		ἄνθρωπος		βιβλίον	
μία	ψυχή	εἷς	ἄνθρωπος	ἕν	βιβλίον
μίαν	ψυχήν	ἑνός	ἀνθρώπου	ἑνί	βιβλίῳ
δυοῖν (gen)	ψυχῶν	δυοῖν (gen)	ἀνθρώπων	δυοῖν (gen)	βιβλίων
δυοῖν (dat)	ψυχαῖς	δυοῖν (dat)	ἀνθρώποις	δυοῖν (dat)	βιβλίοις
τρισίν	ψυχαῖς	τρισίν	ἀνθρώποις	τρισίν	βιβλίοις
τέτταρες	ψυχαί	τέτταρες	ἄνθρωποι	τέτταρα	βιβλία

Note: The final acute accents would become grave if the examples occurred in a sentence.

Identify whether the following English sentences would be expressed by an actual result clause or a natural result clause.

1. Alcibiades drank so much wine that he became sick.
Actual Result

2. Alcibiades drank enough wine to become sick.
Natural Result

3. Alcibiades had the charisma to sway the people.
Natural Result

4. Alcibiades had so much charisma that he swayed the people.
Actual Result

Translate the following sentences into Greek.

¶ ἄνθρωπος, –ου, ὁ = human being, person | ἁμαρτάνω, ἁμαρτήσομαι, ἥμαρτον = to err, sin | ἔχω, ἕξω (or σχήσω), ἔσχον = to have | πλοῦτος, –ου, ὁ = wealth | οὐκέτι (adv.) = no longer

1. No one has so much knowledge that they know nothing.
οὐδεὶς ἔχει τοσαύτην τὴν ἐπιστήμην ὥστε ἐπίσταται οὐδέν.

2. I know one thing. You know two things. We know three things.
ἐπίσταμαι ἕν, ἐπίστασαι δύο, ἐπιστάμεθα τρία.

3. No one has knowledge so as to no longer sin.
οὐδεὶς ἔχει τὴν ἐπιστήμην ὥστε οὐκέτι ἁμαρτάνειν.

4. We had so much wealth that we divided the men.
ἔσχομεν τοσοῦτον τὸν πλοῦτον ὥστε ἐχωρίσαμεν τοὺς ἀνθρώπους.

5. Don't (singular) separate knowledge.
μὴ χώριζε τὴν ἐπιστήμην.

Chapter 23 ∾

1. ἀνδρῶν ἁπάντων Σωκράτης σοφώτατος. (Oracle at Delphi, in Diogenes Laertius, *Lives of Eminent Philosophers*)
Of all men, Socrates is the wisest.
Socrates is the wisest of all men.

2. συγγνώμη τιμωρίας κρείσσων. (Pittacus, in Diogenes Laertius, *Lives of Eminent Philosophers*)
Forgiveness is stronger than vengeance.
Pardon is better than vengeance.
  - κρείσσων, as a comparative of ἀγαθός, can mean "better," but it has the connotation of "stronger." While it might at times be necessary to translate κρείσσων as "better," try "stronger" first.

3. νυνὶ δὲ μένει πίστις, ἐλπίς, ἀγάπη, τὰ τρία ταῦτα· μείζων δὲ τούτων ἡ ἀγάπη. (1 Cor 13:13)
And now remains faith, hope, and love, these three things. But the greater of these is love.
And now faith, hope, and love remain, these three things. But the greatest of these is love.
  - Technically μείζων is a comparative, not a superlative, but it is fine to translate it as a superlative here.

4. οὐκ ἔστι σοφίας κτῆμα τιμιώτερον. (Menander, *Fragments*)
There is not a possession more valuable than wisdom.

There is no possession more valuable than wisdom.

A possession more valuable than wisdom does not exist.

5. ἡ γὰρ ψυχὴ πλεῖόν ἐστιν τῆς τροφῆς καὶ τὸ σῶμα τοῦ ἐνδύματος. (Luke 12:23)

For life is more than food and the body more than clothing.

6. φιλοσόφου τοῦτο τὸ πάθος, τὸ θαυμάζειν· οὐ γὰρ ἄλλη ἀρχὴ φιλοσοφίας ἢ αὕτη. (Socrates, in Plato, *Theatetus*)

This is the experience of the philosopher: wonder. For there is no other beginning of philosophy than this.

This suffering of the philosopher is wonder. For there is no other beginning of philosophy than this beginning.

7. ὑμεῖς δὲ οὐχ οὕτως, ἀλλ᾽ ὁ μείζων ἐν ὑμῖν γινέσθω ὡς ὁ νεώτερος, καὶ ὁ ἡγούμενος ὡς ὁ διακονῶν. (Luke 22:26)

But you, (act) not this way, but let the greater among you become like the younger, and the leader as the one serving.

But don't behave in this way, but let the greater among you be like the lesser, and let the leader be like the servant.

8. ὁ δὲ πολλῷ μᾶλλον ἔκραζεν, "Υἱὲ Δαυίδ, ἐλέησόν με." (Mark 10:48)

But he cried out louder by far, "Son of David, pity me."

But he cried out much more, "Son of David, have mercy on me."

9. βέλτιόν ἐστι τὸ σῶμά γ᾽ ἢ ψυχὴν νοσεῖν. (Menander, *Fragments*)

It is better that the body be sick than the soul.

It is better that the body, rather than the soul, be sick.

10. εἰ γὰρ ἡ διακονία τῆς κατακρίσεως δόξα, πολλῷ μᾶλλον περισσεύει ἡ διακονία τῆς δικαιοσύνης δόξῃ. (2 Cor 3:9)

For if the service of condemnation is glory, how much more does the service of righteousness abound in glory?

For if the ministry of condemnation is glorious, by how much more does the ministry of righteousness overflow in glory?

Supplementary Exercises

Write the corresponding comparative and superlative forms for the following adjectives.

Positive Adjective	Comparative Adjective	Superlative Adjective	Positive Adjective	Comparative Adjective	Superlative Adjective
σοφός	σοφώτερος	σοφώτατος	καλά	καλλίονα / καλλίω	κάλλιστα
σοφή	σοφωτέρα	σοφωτάτη	καλοῦ	καλλίονος	καλλίστου
σοφῷ	σοφωτέρῳ	σοφωτάτῳ	καλάς	καλλίονας	καλλίστας

Write the corresponding comparative and superlative forms for the following adverbs.

PositiveAdverb	Comparative Adverb	Superlative Adverb
σοφῶς	σοφώτερον / μᾶλλον σοφῶς	σαφώτατα / μάλιστα σαφῶς
καλῶς	κάλλιον / μᾶλλον καλῶς	κάλλιστα / μᾶλλον καλῶς
μάλα	μᾶλλον	μάλιστα

Translate the following sentences into Greek.

❡ ἄνθρωπος, –ου, ὁ = human being, person | διδάσκαλος, –ου, ὁ = teacher | εἰμί = to be | ἔχω, ἕξω (or σχήσω), ἔσχον = to have | ὀργή, –ῆς, ἡ = anger | πλοῦτος, –ου, ὁ = wealth | σοφός, –ή, –όν (adj.) = wise | χορτάζω, χορτάσω, ἐχόρτασα = to feed

1. Service is greater than wealth. (Use ἤ.)

ἡ διακονία ἐστὶ μείζων ἢ πλοῦτος.

2. Service is greater than wealth. (Use a genitive of comparison.)

ἡ διακονία ἐστὶ μείζων πλούτου.

3. We know that forgiveness is stronger than anger.

γιγνώσκομεν τὴν συγγνώμην εἶναι κρείττονα (Koine κρείσσονα) ἢ τὴν ὀργήν.

4. I know that experience is the wisest teacher by far.

γιγνώσκω τὸ πάθος εἶναι πολλῷ σοφώτατον διδάσκαλον.

5. Forgiveness fed the people more than possessions.

ἡ συγγνώμη ἐχόρτασε τοὺς ἀνθρώπους μᾶλλον ἢ τὰ κτήματα.

Chapter 24 ⌇

1. σοφία γάρ ἐστι καὶ μαθεῖν ὃ μὴ νοεῖς. (Menander, *Fragments*)
For wisdom is also to know what you do not know.
For it is also wisdom to know that which you do not know.
For wisdom is also to understand what you do not know.

2. ὁ δὲ Ἰησοῦς κάτω κύψας τῷ δακτύλῳ κατέγραφεν εἰς τὴν γῆν. (John 8:6)
And Jesus, having bent down, was writing in the ground with his finger.
And Jesus, having bent down, began to write on the ground with his finger.

- The imperfect can denote the beginning of an action, hence the second translation.

And Jesus bent down and began writing on the ground with his finger.

- For beginning students, I don't recommend translating a circumstantial participle as a finite verb. It is not wrong, but make sure you know the difference between a subordinating participle and the finite verb of a clause.

3. ἰδοὺ γὰρ ἀπὸ τοῦ νῦν μακαριοῦσίν με πᾶσαι αἱ γενεαί. (Luke 1:48)
For behold, from now on all generations will call me fortunate.
For behold, henceforth all generations will call me blessed.

- Notice the liquid future μακαριοῦσίν. It looks like it has two accents, because the enclitic με is throwing its accent back. For more on enclitics, see appendix C.

4. πολλοὶ μὲν εὐτυχοῦσιν, οὐ φρονοῦσι δέ. (Menander, *Fragments*)
Many are fortunate, but they are not wise.
Many are fortunate, but they don't think so.

- Since this is a fragment, it is impossible to know which translation fits the context.

5. ἀνὴρ δὲ χρηστὸς χρηστὸν οὐ μισεῖ ποτε. (Euripides, *Fragments*)
A useful man does not ever hate anything useful.
A good man does not ever hate the good.

6. ἀλλ᾽ εἷς τῶν στρατιωτῶν λόγχῃ αὐτοῦ τὴν πλευρὰν ἔνυξεν, καὶ ἐξῆλθεν εὐθὺς αἷμα καὶ ὕδωρ. (John 19:34)
But one of the soldiers pierced his side with a spear, and immediately blood and water came out.
But one of the soldiers pierced his side with a spear, and at once blood and water poured forth.

7. ἀπεκρίθη Ἰησοῦς καὶ εἶπεν αὐτοῖς, "Λύσατε τὸν ναὸν τοῦτον καὶ ἐν τρισὶν ἡμέραις ἐγερῶ αὐτόν." (John 2:19)
Jesus answered and said to them, "Destroy this temple and in three days I will raise it up."

8. κἀγὼ ὑμῖν λέγω, αἰτεῖτε, καὶ δοθήσεται ὑμῖν· ζητεῖτε, καὶ εὑρήσετε· κρούετε, καὶ ἀνοιγήσεται ὑμῖν. (Luke 11:9)
And I say to you, ask, and it will be given to you, seek, and you will find, knock, and it will be opened to you.

9. νὺξ μὲν ἀναπαύει, ἡμέρα δ᾽ ἔργον ποιεῖ. (Menander, *Fragments*)
Night stops, while day makes work.
Night stops work, but day makes work.

10. καὶ ἐκήρυσσεν λέγων, "Ἔρχεται ὁ ἰσχυρότερός μου ὀπίσω μου, οὗ οὐκ εἰμὶ ἱκανὸς κύψας λῦσαι τὸν ἱμάντα τῶν ὑποδημάτων αὐτοῦ· ἐγὼ ἐβάπτισα ὑμᾶς ὕδατι, αὐτὸς δὲ βαπτίσει ὑμᾶς ἐν πνεύματι ἁγίῳ." (Mark 1:7–8)

And he preached, saying "One stronger than I comes after me, of whom I am unworthy, having bent down, to loosen the strap of his sandals. I baptized you with water, but he will baptize you with the Holy Spirit.

And he preached, saying, "The one stronger than I is coming after me, whose sandals I am unworthy to bend down and untie. I baptized you with water, he will baptize you in the Holy Spirit.

Supplementary Exercises

Write the contracted forms for the following uncontracted forms of φιλέω.

φιλέω	φιλῶ	φιλέεται	φιλεῖται
φίλεε	φίλει	φιλέετε	φιλεῖτε
ἐφιλεόμην	ἐφιλούμην	φιλέουσιν	φιλοῦσιν
ἐφίλεε	ἐφίλει	φιλέειν	φιλεῖν
ἐφιλέομεν	ἐφιλοῦμεν	φιλέεσθαι	φιλεῖσθαι
φιλεόμεθα	φιλούμεθα		

Write the corresponding future active forms of the following present active forms.

Present Active	Future Active	Present Active	Future Active
μένω	μενῶ	βάλλεις	βαλεῖς
μένομεν	μενοῦμεν	βαλλέτω	βαλέτω
μένει	μενεῖ	βάλλει	βαλεῖ

Translate the following sentences into Greek.

1. You (singular) will respond.

ἀποκρινεῖ.

- 2nd person future middle, not 3rd person future active.

2. We baptized the soldiers with water. (Use a dative of means without a preposition.)

ἐβαπτίσαμεν τοὺς στρατιώτας ὕδατι.

ἐβαπτίσαμεν τοὺς στρατιώτας τῷ ὕδατι.

3. We baptized the soldiers with water. (Use ἐν + dative.)

ἐβαπτίσαμεν τοὺς στρατιώτας ἐν ὕδατι.

4. Let the temple be found.

εὑρισκέσθω ὁ ναός.

5. The soldiers were thinking that they were wise.

οἱ στρατιῶται ἐνόουν ὅτι αὐτοί εἰσι σοφοί.

- The use of the intensive αὐτοὶ is not strictly necessary.

οἱ στρατιῶται ἐνόουν εἶναι σοφοί.

- Remember that in indirect statement with the accusative + infinitive, the exception to the subject being in the accusative is when the subject of the indirect statement is the subject of the verb that introduces the indirect statement, as is the case here.

6. I hate and I love.

μισῶ καὶ φιλῶ.

7. You (plural) will not find water at once.

οὐχ εὑρήσετε τὸ ὕδωρ εὐθύς.

Chapter 25 ∽

1. ζῶ δὲ οὐκέτι ἐγώ, ζῇ δὲ ἐν ἐμοὶ Χριστός. (Gal 2:20)
But I no longer live, but Christ lives in me.
It is no longer I who live, but Christ lives in me.

2. μὴ νικῶ ὑπὸ τοῦ κακοῦ, ἀλλὰ νίκα ἐν τῷ ἀγαθῷ τὸ κακόν. (Rom 12:21)
Do not be conquered by evil, but conquer evil with good.

3. ἐρωτηθεὶς ποῖον οἶνον ἡδέως πίνει, ὁ Διογένης ἔφη, "τὸν ἀλλότριον."
(Diogenes the Cynic, in Diogenes Laertius, *Lives of Eminent Philosophers*)
Having been asked what sort of wine he pleasurably drank, Diogenes said,
"that belonging to another."
Being asked what kind of wine he most enjoyed, Diogenes said "someone
else's."
- Notice the use of the present tense in the indirect question.
  Because English changes the tense of subordinate clauses if intro-
  duced by a past tense verb, it sounds best to translate πίνει as a past
  tense.

4. λέγει αὐτῷ ὁ Πιλᾶτος, "Τί ἐστιν ἀλήθεια;" (John 18:38)
Pilate says to him, "What is truth?"

5. τίς ἡμᾶς χωρίσει ἀπὸ τῆς ἀγάπης τοῦ Χριστοῦ; (Rom 8:35)
Who will separate us from the love of Christ?

6. οὐδὲν ὁ Θαλῆς ἔφη τὸν θάνατον διαφέρειν τοῦ ζῆν. "σὺ," ἔφη τις, "διὰ τί οὐκ ἀποθνήσκεις;" "ὅτι," ἔφη, "οὐδὲν διαφέρει." (Thales, in Diogenes Laertius, *Lives of Eminent Philosophers*)

Thales said that death is different than life in no way. Someone said, "Why don't you die?" "Because," he said, "In no way is it different."

Thales said that death was different than life in no way. Someone said, "Why don't you die?" "Because," he said, "In no way is it different."

Thales said that death differs from life in no way. "Then why don't YOU kill yourself," someone said. Thales said, "Because it differs in no way."

- The personal pronoun σὺ, while not grammatically necessary, adds emphasis. It can sometimes be tricky to translate emphatic pronouns in English.

7. ὧν ἕνεκα ζῆν ἐθέλεις, τούτων χάριν καὶ ἀποθανεῖν μὴ κατόκνει. (Pythagoras, in Stobaeus, *Anthology*)

For the sake of which you want to live, for the sake of these things do not shrink back from dying.

For the sake of the things for which you want to live, do not hesitate also to die for these things.

8. μήτε νέος μελλέτω φιλοσοφεῖν, μήτε γέρων κοπιάτω φιλοσοφῶν. (Epicurus, *Letter to Menoeceus*)

Let the young neither hesitate to philosophize, nor let the old grow tired of philosophizing.

Let the young person neither hesitate to philosophize, nor let the old grow tired of philosophizing.

9. ὡς κύκλος τῶν ἀνθρώπων ἐστὶ πράγματα, περιφερόμενος δὲ οὐκ ἐᾷ ἀεὶ τοὺς αὐτοὺς εὐτυχεῖν. (Herodotus, *Histories*)

Like a circle are the matters of humans, and revolving it does not allow the same people to always prosper.

Like a wheel are the affairs of men, and turning it does not always allow the same men to prosper.

10. εἶπεν δὲ αὐτοῖς, "Ὑμεῖς δὲ τίνα με λέγετε εἶναι;" Πέτρος δὲ ἀποκριθεὶς εἶπεν,
"Τὸν Χριστὸν τοῦ θεοῦ." (Luke 9:20)
And he said to them, "But you, whom do you say that I am?" And Peter,
responding, said "The anointed one of God."
And he said to them, "But whom do you say that I am?" And Peter
responded and said to him, "The Messiah of God."

Supplementary Exercises

Write the contracted forms for the following uncontracted forms of
νικάω.

νικάομαι	νικῶμαι	ἐνικάεσθε	ἐνικᾶσθε
νικάει	νικᾷ	νικαέσθων	νικάσθων
νικάομεν	νικῶμεν	νικαέτω	νικάτω
ἐνίκαε	ἐνίκα	νικάεσθαι	νικᾶσθαι
ἐνίκαον	ἐνίκων	νικάειν	νικᾶν
ἐνικάοντο	ἐνικῶντο		

Indicate whether the following forms are interrogative pronouns or indefinite pronouns.

τις	indefinite	τίσιν	interrogative
του	indefinite	τίνος	interrogative
τίς	interrogative	τι	indefinite
τινά	indefinite	τοῦ	interrogative
τινῶν	indefinite	ἄττα	indefinite

Translate the following sentences into Greek.
¶ διδάσκαλος, –ου, ὁ = teacher | ὀργή, –ῆς, ἡ = anger | σοφός, –ή, –όν
(adj.) = wise

1. Why do we philosophize?

τί φιλοσοφοῦμεν;

2. Let the wise man conquer anger.

νικάτω ὁ σοφὸς τὴν ὀργήν.

ὁ σοφὸς νικάτω τὴν ὀργήν.

3. What teacher does not question?

τίς διδάσκαλος οὐκ ἐρωτᾷ;

4. Certain teachers neither question nor philosophize.

τινὲς διδάσκαλοι οὔτε ἐρωτῶσιν οὔτε φιλοσοφοῦσιν.

5. Philosophize (plural) and prosper!

φιλοσοφεῖτε καὶ εὐτυχεῖτε.

Chapter 26 〜

1. ἡ γνῶσις φυσιοῖ, ἡ δὲ ἀγάπη οἰκοδομεῖ. (1 Cor 8:1)
Knowledge puffs up, but love builds up.

2. μικρὰ ζύμη ὅλον τὸ φύραμα ζυμοῖ. (Gal 5:9)
A little leaven leavens the whole dough.
A little amount of leaven makes the whole dough rise.

3. φίλτατος εἶ καὶ ἀληθῶς χρυσοῦς, ὦ Φαῖδρε, εἴ με οἴει λέγειν ὡς Λυσίας. (Socrates, in Plato, *Phaedrus*)
You are dearest and truly golden, oh Phaedrus, if you think that I speak like Lysias.
You are the dearest and truly golden, oh Phaedrus, if you believe that I speak like Lysias.
- Notice the indirect statement with the accusative + infinitive construction.

4. ὁ θάνατος οὐδὲν πρὸς ἡμᾶς· τὸ γὰρ διαλυθὲν ἀναισθητεῖ, τὸ δ᾽ ἀναισθητοῦν οὐδὲν πρὸς ἡμᾶς. (Epicurus, in Diogenes Laertius, *Lives of Eminent Philosophers*)
Death is nothing to us. For that which is destroyed lacks perception, but that which lacks perception is nothing to us.
Death is irrelevant to us. Something destroyed does not perceive, and something that does not perceive is irrelevant to us.

5. διπλῶς ὁρῶσιν οἱ μαθόντες γράμματα. (Menander, *Fragments*)

Those having learned letters see double.

Those who know letters see twice.

They see twice who know how to read.

6. ἀλλὰ ὑμῖν λέγω τοῖς ἀκούουσιν, ἀγαπᾶτε τοὺς ἐχθροὺς ὑμῶν, καλῶς ποιεῖτε τοῖς μισοῦσιν ὑμᾶς. (Luke 6:27)

But I say to you listening, love your enemies, do well to those hating you.

And I say to you who hear, love your enemies, act nobly to those who hate you.

7. καὶ εἰ ἀγαπᾶτε τοὺς ἀγαπῶντας ὑμᾶς, ποία ὑμῖν χάρις ἐστίν; καὶ γὰρ οἱ ἁμαρτωλοὶ τοὺς ἀγαπῶντας αὐτοὺς ἀγαπῶσιν. (Luke 6:32)

And if you love those loving you, what kind of grace is that for you? For indeed, sinners love those loving them.

And if you love those who love you, what sort of grace is yours? For indeed, sinners love those who love them.

8. ἀεὶ τὸ λυποῦν ἐκδίωκε τοῦ βίου. (Menander, *Fragments*)

Always banish what causes grief from life.

Always banish that which causes grief from life.

Always banish grief from your life.

- Sometimes translating substantive nouns formed from attributive participles is tricky.

9. Βίων ἔλεγε κατὰ Ἡσίοδον τρία γένη εἶναι μαθητῶν: χρυσοῦν, ἀργυροῦν, χαλκοῦν· χρυσοῦν μὲν τὸ γένος τῶν διδόντων καὶ μανθανόντων· ἀργυροῦν δὲ τὸ γένος τῶν διδόντων καὶ μὴ μανθανόντων· χαλκοῦν δὲ τὸ γένος τῶν μανθανόντων μέν, οὐ διδόντων δέ. (Bion, in Diogenes Laertius, *Lives of Eminent Philosophers*)

Bion used to say that, in accordance with Hesiod, there are three types of students: gold, silver, bronze. Gold is the type of those paying and learning, silver is the type of those paying and not learning, and bronze is the type of those learning, but not paying.

10. καὶ ἰδοὺ ἄνθρωπος ἦν ἐν Ἰερουσαλὴμ ᾧ ὄνομα Συμεών, καὶ ὁ ἄνθρωπος οὗτος δίκαιος καὶ εὐλαβής, προσδεχόμενος παράκλησιν τοῦ Ἰσραήλ, καὶ πνεῦμα ἦν ἅγιον ἐπ᾽ αὐτόν. (Luke 2:25)

And behold, there was a man in Jerusalem whose name was Simeon, and this man was just and pious, awaiting the consolation of Israel, and the Holy Spirit was upon him.

Supplementary Exercises

Write the contracted forms for the following uncontracted forms of δηλόω.

δηλόω	δηλῶ	δηλοέτω	δηλούτω
δηλόομαι	δηλοῦμαι	δηλόου	δηλοῦ
δηλόουσι	δηλοῦσι	δήλοε	δήλου
ἐδηλοόμην	ἐδηλούμην	δηλόεσθαι	δηλοῦσθαι
ἐδηλόομεν	ἐδηλοῦμεν	δηλόειν	δηλοῦν
ἐδήλοον	ἐδήλουν		

Translate the following sentences into Greek.

¶ διδάσκαλος, -ου, ὁ = teacher | εἰμί = to be

1. Knowledge is golden.
ἡ γνῶσίς ἐστι χρυσοῦς.

2. The knowledge of the teacher is small. (Use a genitive of possession.)
ἡ γνῶσις τοῦ διδασκάλου ἐστὶ μικρά.

3. The knowledge of the teacher is small. (Use a dative of possession.)
ἡ γνῶσις τῷ διδασκάλῳ ἐστὶ μικρά.

4. The enemies made themselves known.
οἱ ἐχθροὶ ἐδηλοῦντο.

5. We will reveal the small things to the enemy.

δηλώσομεν τὰ μικρὰ τῷ ἐχθρῷ.

6. I think that the teachers will not see golden things.

οἴομαι ὅτι οἱ διδάσκαλοι οὐκ βλέψονται τὰ χρύσεα.

βλέπω is a future deponent, hence βλέψονται.

7. Let knowledge be loved.

ἀγαπάσθω ἡ γνῶσις.

ἡ γνῶσις ἀγαπάσθω.

Chapter 27 ~

1. μετανοεῖτε, ἤγγικεν γὰρ ἡ βασιλεία τῶν οὐρανῶν. (Matthew 3:2)
Change your thinking, for the kingdom of heaven has approached.
Repent, for the kingdom of heaven is imminent.

- If you can translate a perfect verb with "has/have...," that is usually the best. Sometimes it sounds awkward and using the present tense is best. Keep in mind, however, that the perfect depicts an action that is completed, but has bearing on the present.

2. οὐδεὶς ὃ νοεῖς μὲν οἶδεν, ὃ δὲ ποιεῖς βλέπει. (Menander, *Fragments*)
No one knows what you are thinking, but they do see what you are doing.
No one knows what you think, but everyone sees what you do.

3. ἐν τῷ κόσμῳ θλῖψιν ἔχετε, ἀλλὰ θαρσεῖτε, ἐγὼ νενίκηκα τὸν κόσμον. (John 16:33)
You have affliction in the world, but have courage, I have conquered the world.

4. εἶπεν δὲ πρὸς τὴν γυναῖκα, "Ἡ πίστις σου σέσωκέν σε· πορεύου εἰς εἰρήνην." (Luke 7:50)
And he said to the woman, "Your faith has saved you. Go in peace."

5. κἀγὼ ἑώρακα, καὶ μεμαρτύρηκα ὅτι οὗτός ἐστιν ὁ υἱὸς τοῦ θεοῦ. (John 1:34)
And I have seen, and I have testified that this one is the son of God.
I have seen and witnessed that this is the son of God.

6. θνητὸς γεγονώς, ἄνθρωπε, μὴ φρόνει μέγα. (Menander, *Fragments*)
Having become mortal, human, do not think great things.
Being mortal, human, don't think great things.
Since you are a mortal, human, don't think great things.

7. ὁ δὲ λέγων ἢ μήπω τοῦ φιλοσοφεῖν ὑπάρχειν ὥραν ἢ παρεληλυθέναι τὴν
ὥραν ὅμοιός ἐστι τῷ λέγοντι πρὸς εὐδαιμονίαν ἢ μὴ παρεῖναι τὴν ὥραν ἢ
μηκέτι εἶναι. (Epicurus, *Letter to Menoeceus*)
And the one saying it is not yet time to philosophize, or that the time has passed,
is like one saying that, for happiness, it is not time or it is no longer time.
But the one who says that it is not yet time to practice philosophy, or that
the time has passed, is like one who says it is not time for happiness, or
that it is no longer time for happiness.

8. ἄνδρες Ἀθηναῖοι, τῶν μὲν σοφώτερος, τῶν δὲ ἀνδρειότερός εἰμι· σοφώτερος
μὲν τῶν τὴν ἀπάτην Πεισιστράτου μὴ συνιέντων, ἀνδρειότερος δὲ τῶν
ἐπισταμένων μέν, διὰ δέος δὲ σιωπώντων. (Solon, in Diogenes Laertius,
Lives of Eminent Philosophers)
Athenian men, I am wiser than some, and more courageous than others.
I am wiser than those not knowing the deceit of Peisistratus, and more
courageous than to who know, but remain silent on account of fear.
 • The τῶν μὲν ... τῶν δὲ here is just the οἱ μὲν ... οἱ δὲ (some ... others)
   construction in the genitive case on account of the genitive of
   comparison.

9. οὐκ οἴδατε ὅτι ναὸς θεοῦ ἐστε καὶ τὸ πνεῦμα τοῦ θεοῦ οἰκεῖ ἐν ὑμῖν; (1 Cor
3:16)
Do you not know that you are a temple of God and that the Spirit of God
dwells within you?

10. ὅτε ἤμην νήπιος, ἐλάλουν ὡς νήπιος, ἐφρόνουν ὡς νήπιος, ἐλογιζόμην ὡς
νήπιος· ὅτε γέγονα ἀνήρ, κατήργηκα τὰ τοῦ νηπίου. (1 Cor 13:11)
When I was a child, I used to speak like a child, think like a child, and
reason like a child. Since I have become a man, I have put aside the things
of a child.

Supplementary Exercises

Give the person and number of the following perfect active forms of λύω.

Person	Number		Person	Number	
λελύκαμεν	1	Plural	λέλυκας	2	Singular
λέλυκα	1	Singular	λελύκασιν	3	Plural
λέλυκεν	3	Singular	λελύκατε	2	Plural

Give the corresponding forms of the definite article and perfect active participle of λύω.

❡ βιβλίον, –ου, ὁ = book | δεσμός, –οῦ, ὁ = chain | χαρά, –ᾶς, ἡ = joy

Definite Article	Perfect Active Participle of λύω	
ὁ	λελυκὼς	δεσμός
τοὺς	λελυκότας	δεσμούς
τοῖς	λελυκόσι(ν)	δεσμοῖς
τῆς	λελυκυίας	χαρᾶς
τάς	λελυκυίας	χαράς
τῶν	λελυκότων / λελυκυιῶν	χαρῶν
τὸ	λελυκὸς	βιβλίον
τὰ	λελυκότα	βιβλία
τοῦ	λελυκότος	βιβλίου

Give the person, number, and mood of the following forms of οἶδα.

	Person	Number	Mood		Person	Number	Mood
οἶδεν	3	Singular	Indicative	ἴστων	3	Plural	Imperative
οἶσθα	2	Singular	Indicative	ἴστω	3	Singular	Imperative
ἴσασιν	3	Plural	Indicative	ἴστε	2	Plural	Indicative
ἴσθι	2	Singular	Imperative	ἴστε	2	Plural	Imperative
οἶδα	1	Singular	Indicative	ἴσμεν	1	Plural	Indicative

Translate the following sentences into Greek.

εἰμί = to be | ἐν (prep.) = in (+ dative) | ζωή, –ῆς, ἡ = life |
τίς, τί (interrogative pronoun) = who, what

1. Is there happiness in life?
ἔστι ἡ εὐδαιμονία ἐν ζωῇ;

2. Say (singular) what life is.
λέγε τί ἐστι ἡ ζωή.

3. Have you (singular) changed your mind?
μετανενόηκας;

4. Let the mortals know peace!
οἱ θνητοὶ ἴστων τὴν εἰρήνην.

5. I do not know what is similar to peace.
οὐκ οἶδα τί ἐστι ὅμοιον τῇ εἰρήνῃ.

6. We think that the hour of happiness has approached.
λογιζόμεθα ὅτι ἡ ὥρα τῆς εὐδαιμονίας ἤγγικεν.

7. You (singular) have not testified.
οὐ μεμαρτύρηκας.

8. I know that the mortals have not lived in peace.
οἶδα ὅτι οἱ θνητοὶ οὐκ ᾠκήκασιν ἐν εἰρήνῃ.

Chapter 28 ~

1. τὸν καλὸν ἀγῶνα ἠγώνισμαι, τὸν δρόμον τετέλεκα, τὴν πίστιν τετήρηκα. (2 Tim. 4:7)
I have fought the noble contest. I have completed the course. I have kept the faith.
I have fought the good fight. I have finished the race. I have kept the faith.

2. βλέπων πεπαίδευμ᾽ εἰς τὰ τῶν πολλῶν κακά. (Menander, *Fragments*)
I have become educated looking at the evils of many men.
I have become educated by looking at the evils of many things.
   - Because this is a fragment and we don't know the context, τῶν πολλῶν could be masculine plural or neuter plural.

3. Λάζαρος ὁ φίλος ἡμῶν κεκοίμηται. (John 11:11)
Lazarus our friend has died.
Our friend Lazarus has died.

4. θνητὸς πεφυκὼς μὴ γέλα τεθνηκότα. (Menander, *Fragments*)
Having been born mortal, do not mock one who has died.
Since you were born mortal, do not mock the dead.

5. ἡ εὐτραπελία πεπαιδευμένη ὕβρις ἐστίν. (Aristotle, *Rhetoric*)
Wit is educated hubris.
Wit is educated pride.
   - While grammatically πεπαιδευμένη could modify ὕβρις, the sense dictates that it modify εὐτραπελία.

6. τῇ γὰρ χάριτί ἐστε σεσῳσμένοι διὰ πίστεως· καὶ τοῦτο οὐκ ἐξ ὑμῶν, θεοῦ τὸ δῶρον. (Eph 2:8)

For you have been saved through faith by grace, and this is not from you, but a gift of God.

For you have been saved through faith by grace, and this is not from you, but it is a gift of God.

7. ὁ τῆς φύσεως πλοῦτος καὶ ὥρισται καὶ εὐπόριστός ἐστιν, ὁ δὲ τῶν κενῶν δοξῶν εἰς ἄπειρον ἐκπίπτει. (Epicurus, in Diogenes Laertius, *Lives of Eminent Philosophers*)

The wealth of nature is both defined and easy to secure, but the wealth of empty glories issues forth into the infinite.

The wealth of nature is both limited and easy to secure, but the wealth of empty opinions rushes out into the infinite.

8. ἀλλὰ καὶ αἱ τρίχες τῆς κεφαλῆς ὑμῶν πᾶσαι ἠρίθμηνται. μὴ φοβεῖσθε. (Luke 12:7)

And even the hairs of your head, all of them have been numbered. Do not be afraid.

And even all the hairs of your head have been numbered. Do not be afraid.

9. εἰ γὰρ ἐχθροὶ ὄντες κατηλλάγημεν τῷ θεῷ διὰ τοῦ θανάτου τοῦ υἱοῦ αὐτοῦ, πολλῷ μᾶλλον καταλλαγέντες σωθησόμεθα ἐν τῇ ζωῇ αὐτοῦ. (Rom 5:10)

For if, being enemies, we have been reconciled to God through the death of his son, by how much more, being reconciled, will we be saved in his life.

For if, when we were enemies, we were reconciled to God by his death, by how much more, since we are reconciled, will we be saved by his life.

10. ἐρωτηθεὶς τίνι διαφέρουσιν οἱ πεπαιδευμένοι τῶν ἀπαιδεύτων, "ὅσῳ," εἶπεν, "οἱ ζῶντες τῶν τεθνεώτων." (Aristotle, in Diogenes Laertius, *Lives of Eminent Philosophers*)

Having been asked by how much the educated differ from the uneducated, he said "By as much as the living from the dead."

When he was asked by how much those who have been educated differed from the uneducated, he said, "By as much as the living differ from those who have died."

Supplementary Exercises

Give all six principal parts of your model verb λύω.

1	2	3	4	5	6
present active	future active	aorist active	perfect active	perfect m/p	aorist passive
λύω	λύσω	ἔλυσα	λέλυκα	λέλυμαι	ἐλύθην

Write the primary and secondary middle/passive endings.

	Primary Middle/ Passive Endings			Secondary Middle/ Passive Endings	
	Singular	Plural		Singular	Plural
1st	μαι	μεθα	1st	μην	μεθα
2nd	σαι	σθε	2nd	σο	σθε
3rd	ται	νται	3rd	το	ντο

Translate the following sentences into Greek.

¶ εἰμί = to be | ὑπό (ὑπ᾽/ὑφ᾽) (prep.) = under, by (+ gen.)

1. The struggle is not fulfilled by violence.

ὁ ἀγὼν οὐ τελεῖται ὑφ᾽ ὕβρεως.

ὁ ἀγὼν οὐ τελεῖται ὑπὸ τῆς ὕβρεως.

2. The struggle has not been fulfilled by violence.

ὁ ἀγὼν οὐ τετέλεσται ὑφ᾽ ὕβρεως.

ὁ ἀγὼν οὐ τετέλεσται ὑπὸ τῆς ὕβρεως.

3. Infinite violence grows.

ὁ ἄπειρος ὕβρις φύεται.

- ἄπειρος, -ον does not have separate feminine forms.

4. Be (plural) not afraid.

μὴ φοβεῖσθε.

5. Nature has not been protected by arrogance.

ἡ φύσις οὐ τετήρηται ὑφ' ὕβρεως.

6. We will complete the struggle.

τελέσομεν τὸν ἀγῶνα.

Chapter 29 ⁓

1. γνῶθι σαυτόν. (Oracle at Delphi)
Know yourself.
Know thyself.

2. καὶ οὐδεὶς ἐπίασεν αὐτόν, ὅτι οὔπω ἐληλύθει ἡ ὥρα αὐτοῦ. (John 8:20)
And no one arrested him, because his hour had not yet come.
But no one arrested him, because his hour had not yet arrived.

3. ὁ σοφὸς ἐν αὐτῷ περιφέρει τὴν οὐσίαν. (Menander, *Fragments*)
The wise man carries wealth in himself.

4. Ῥαδάμανθυς ἀγαθὸς ἦν ἀνήρ· ἐπεπαίδευτο γὰρ ὑπὸ τοῦ Μίνωος. (Plato, *Minos*)
Rhadamanthus was a good man. For he had been educated by Minos.

5. ἡνίκα δὲ Φίλιππος ἐτεθνήκει, ὁ Δημοσθένης λαμπρὰν ἐσθῆτα προῆλθεν ἔχων. (Plutarch, *Lives of the Ten Orators*)
And when Phillip had died, Demosthenes went out wearing a shining garment.
And when Phillip had died, Demosthenes presented himself wearing a splendid garment.

6. ὁ γὰρ πᾶς νόμος ἐν ἑνὶ λόγῳ πεπλήρωται, ἐν τῷ ῾Αγαπήσεις τὸν πλησίον σου ὡς σεαυτόν.᾿ (Gal 5:14)

119

For all the law has been fulfilled in one word, in "You will love your neighbor as yourself."

For the whole law is fulfilled in one word, in "You will love your neighbor as yourself."

- As an action that has been completed but has bearing on the present, sometimes the present passive can be used to translate the perfect passive.

7. πρᾶττε τὰ σαυτοῦ, μὴ τὰ τῶν ἄλλων φρόνει. (Menander, *Fragments*)
Do the things of yourself, think not about the things of others.
Do your own affairs, do not think about the affairs of others.

8. ἀμὴν λέγω ὑμῖν, ὅσα ἐὰν δήσητε ἐπὶ τῆς γῆς ἔσται δεδεμένα ἐν οὐρανῷ καὶ ὅσα ἐὰν λύσητε ἐπὶ τῆς γῆς ἔσται λελυμένα ἐν οὐρανῷ. (Matthew 18:18)
Amen I say to you, as many things as you bind on earth will have been bound in heaven, and as many things as you loosen on earth will have been loosened in heaven.

9. ἔλεγεν οὖν, "Τίνι ὁμοία ἐστὶν ἡ βασιλεία τοῦ θεοῦ, καὶ τίνι ὁμοιώσω αὐτήν; ὁμοία ἐστὶν κόκκῳ σινάπεως, ὃν λαβὼν ἄνθρωπος ἔβαλεν εἰς κῆπον ἑαυτοῦ, καὶ ηὔξησεν καὶ ἐγένετο εἰς δένδρον, καὶ τὰ πετεινὰ τοῦ οὐρανοῦ κατεσκήνωσεν ἐν τοῖς κλάδοις αὐτοῦ." (Luke 13:18–19)
And he used to say, "To what is the kingdom of heaven similar, and to what shall I compare it? It is like a grain of mustard, which a man, taking, threw into his garden, and it grew and became a tree, and the birds of the sky settled in its branches."

And he said, "What is the kingdom of heaven like, and to what shall I compare it? It is like a seed of mustard, which a man took and threw into his garden, and it grew and became a tree, and the birds of the sky settled in its branches."

10. τὸ γνῶθι σαυτὸν πᾶσίν ἐστι χρήσιμον. (Menander, *Fragments*)
To know yourself is useful for all.
The maxim "Know thyself" is useful for everyone.

Supplementary Exercises

Write the shortened forms of the following reflexive pronouns.

σεαυτοῦ	σαυτοῦ	ἑαυτοῦ	αὑτοῦ
σεαυτόν	σαυτόν	ἑαυτῆς	αὑτῆς
σεαυτῇ	σαυτῇ	ἑαυτήν	αὑτήν
ἑαυτό	αὑτό	ἑαυτῷ	αὑτῷ

Translate the following sentences into Greek.

εἰμί = to be | λέγω, ἐρῶ (or λέξω), εἶπον, εἴρηκα, εἴρημαι (or λέλεγμαι), ἐρρήθην (or λέλειμαι) = to say, speak | μαθητής, –οῦ, ὁ = student | παιδεύω, παιδεύσω, ἐπαίδευσα, πεπαίδευκα, πεπαίδευμαι, ἐπαιδεύθην = to teach | ποῖος, –α, –ον = what kind?, what sort? | πόσος, –η, –ον = how many?, how much? | Σωκράτης, –ους, ὁ = Socrates

1. When Socrates had spoken, he was bound.

ὅτε ὁ Σωκράτης εἰρήκειν, ἐλύθη.

2. When Socrates goes out, he will have taught the students.

ὅτε ὁ Σωκράτης προελεύσεται, πεπαιδευκὼς ἔσται τοὺς μαθητάς.

- In the protasis (if clause) of future conditions, English uses the present tense, while Greek logically prefers the future tense.

3. We did not say what sort of students Socrates had taught.

οὐκ εἴπομεν ποίους μαθητὰς ὁ Σωκράτης ἐπεπαιδεύκειν.

4. How many students will Socrates have taught when we go out?

πόσους μαθητὰς ὁ Σωκράτης πεπαιδευκὼς ἔσται ὅτε προελευσόμεθα;

5. What sort of things have you (plural) taught yourself?

ποῖα ὑμᾶς αὐτοὺς πεπαιδεύκατε; (if the subject is male or a group of male and female)

ποῖα ὑμᾶς αὐτὰς πεπαιδεύκατε; (if the subject is female)

6. The neighbors bound themselves.
οἱ πλησίοι ὑμᾶς αὐτοὺς ἔλυσαν.
οἱ πλησίοι ὑμᾶς αὐτοὺς ἔλυσαν.

7. Fulfill (singular) yourself.
πλήρου σεαυτόν. (male)
πλήρου σαυτόν. (male)
πλήρου σεαυτήν. (female)
πλήρου σαυτήν. (female)

Chapter 30 ～'

1. ὁ Ἀριστοτέλης ἔν τοῖς φυσικοῖς αἰτιολογικώτατος πάντων ἐγένετο ὥστε καὶ περὶ τῶν ἐλαχίστων τὰς αἰτίας ἀποδιδόναι. (Diogenes Laertius, *Lives of Eminent Philosophers*)

Aristotle in the physics was so inquisitive of causes as to define the causes of even the smallest things.

Aristotle in the physics was so curious about causes that he explained the causes of even the smallest things.

- Natural result clauses technically say that a result would naturally follow, while actual result clauses say that a result did in fact follow. As we have seen, often a natural result clause will be used to describe a result that did in fact happen, as was natural. In such cases it can be best to translate them as actual result clauses, as in the second translation.

2. ἐγώ εἰμι ὁ ποιμὴν ὁ καλός, ὁ ποιμὴν ὁ καλὸς τὴν ψυχὴν αὐτοῦ τίθησιν ὑπὲρ τῶν προβάτων. (John 10:11)

I am the noble shepherd, the noble shepherd lays down his life on behalf of the sheep.

I am the good shepherd, the good shepherd lays down his life for the sake of his sheep.

3. ὁ Ἰησοῦς ἐταράχθη τῷ πνεύματι καὶ ἐμαρτύρησεν καὶ εἶπεν, "Ἀμὴν ἀμὴν λέγω ὑμῖν ὅτι εἷς ἐξ ὑμῶν παραδώσει με." (John 13:21)

Jesus was shaken in his spirit and testified and said, "Amen, amen I say to you that one of you will betray me."

4. ἐντολὴν καινὴν δίδωμι ὑμῖν, ἵνα ἀγαπᾶτε ἀλλήλους. (John 13:34)

A new commandment I give to you, that you love each other.

I give you a new commandment, that you love one another.

5. εἰρήνην ἀφίημι ὑμῖν, εἰρήνην τὴν ἐμὴν δίδωμι ὑμῖν· οὐ καθὼς ὁ κόσμος δίδωσιν ἐγὼ δίδωμι ὑμῖν. μὴ ταρασσέσθω ὑμῶν ἡ καρδία μηδὲ δειλιάτω. (John 14:27)

Peace I release to you, my peace I give to you. Not as the world gives do I give to you. Let your heart not be shaken nor be afraid.

Peace I give to you, my peace I give you. Not as the world gives do I give to you. Let your heart not be disturbed nor be in fear.

- While it is not incorrect, I think that "disturbed" is a little too weak of a translation for ταράσσω.

6. ἀναστήσω αὐτὸν ἐν τῇ ἐσχάτῃ ἡμέρᾳ. (John 6:44)

I will raise him up on the last day.

- Notice the transitive, not intransitive, nature of the future tense here.

7. θεὸς δὲ τοῖς ἀργοῖσιν οὐ παρίσταται. (Menander, *Fragments*)

God does not assist the lazy.

A god does not assist the lazy.

- Because this is a fragment, we cannot tell whether the speaker had a specific god in mind.

8. ἡ μωρία δίδωσιν ἀνθρώποις κακά. (Menander, *Fragments*)

Foolishness gives evil things to men.

Foolishness gives evil to humans.

9. καίτοι τί κλέος εὐκλεέστερόν ἐστιν ἢ τὸν αὐτάδελφον ἐν τάφῳ τιθεῖσα; (Sophocles, *Antigone*)

Indeed, what more glorious glory is there than placing one's own brother in the grave?

10. φῶς ἱλαρὸν ἁγίας δόξης ἀθανάτου Πατρός, οὐρανίου, ἁγίου, μάκαρος, Ἰησοῦ Χριστέ, ἐλθόντες ἐπὶ τὴν ἡλίου δύσιν, ἰδόντες φῶς ἑσπερινόν, ὑμνοῦμεν Πατέρα, Υἱόν, καὶ ἅγιον Πνεῦμα, Θεόν. ἄξιόν σε ἐν πᾶσι καιροῖς ὑμνεῖσθαι φωναῖς αἰσίαις, Υἱὲ Θεοῦ, ζωὴν ὁ διδούς· διὸ ὁ κόσμος σὲ δοξάζει. (early Christian hymn)

Oh cheerful light of the holy glory of the immortal Father, heavenly, holy, blessed, Jesus Christ. Coming to the setting of the sun, seeing the evening light, we hymn the Father, Son, and Holy Spirit, God. It is right to hymn you at all times with auspicious voices, Son of God, who gives life. Wherefore the world glorifies you.

- Heavenly, holy, and blessed modify Father, not Jesus. Jesus is in apposition to light.

Oh gladdening light of the holy glory of the immortal, heavenly, holy, and blessed Father, Jesus Christ. When we come to the setting of the sun and see the evening light, we sing a hymn to the Father, the Son, and the Holy Spirit, who are God. It is right that we sing a hymn to you at all times with auspicious words, Son of God, you who give life. For this reason, the universe glorifies you.

Supplementary Exercises

Write the forms of your three model μι verbs for the following:

	δίδωμι	τίθημι	ἵστημι
1st pers., sg., present, act., ind.	δίδωμι	τίθημι	ἵστημι
2nd pers., sg., present, act., imp.	δίδου	τίθει	ἵστη
3rd pers., sg., present, m/p, ind.	δίδοται	τίθεται	ἵσταται
1st pers., pl., present, m/p., ind.	διδόμεθα	τιθέμεθα	ἱστάμεθα
present active infinitive	διδόναι	τιθέναι	ἱστάναι
present middle/passive infinitive	δίδοσθαι	τίθεσθαι	ἵστασθαι

Identify the gender, number, case, tense, and voice of the following participles.

	Gender	Number	Case	Tense	Voice
διδούς	masculine	plural	accusative	present	active
διδομένην	feminine	singular	accusative	present	middle/ passive
τιθέμενοι	masculine	plural	nominative	present	middle/ passive
τιθέν	neuter	singular	nominative	present	active
	neuter	singular	accusative	present	active
ἱστάν	neuter	singular	nominative	present	active
	neuter	singular	accusative	present	active

Translate the following sentences into Greek.
βούλομαι = to want | θεός, –οῦ, ὁ = a god, God

1. The shepherds were giving glory to God.
οἱ ποιμένες ἐδίδοντο τῷ θεῷ.

2. Don't (singular) place blame on the shepherds.
μὴ τίθει αἰτίαν ἐπὶ τοὺς ποιμένας.

3. I will not betray the commandments being given.
οὐκ παραδώσω τὰς διδομένας ἐντολάς.

4. We do not want to place blame.
οὐκ βουλόμεθα τιθέναι τὴν αἰτίαν.

5. A god is standing the shepherd up.
ὁ θεὸς ἵστησι τὸν ποιμένα.

Chapter 31 ～

1. ὁ νόμος διὰ Μωϋσέως ἐδόθη, ἡ χάρις καὶ ἡ ἀλήθεια διὰ Ἰησοῦ Χριστοῦ. (John 1:17)
The law was given through Moses; grace and truth through Jesus Christ.
The law was given through Moses; grace and truth came through Jesus Christ.

2. Ἰησοῦς εἶπεν, "Τετέλεσται," καὶ κλίνας τὴν κεφαλὴν παρέδωκεν τὸ πνεῦμα. (John 19:30)
Jesus said, "It has been fulfilled," and bowing his head he surrendered his spirit.
Jesus said, "It has been finished," and he bowed his head and gave up his spirit.
Jesus said, "It is finished," and bowing his head he gave up his spirit.

- Τετέλεσται is perfect passive, not present passive. As we have seen, however, the nature of the perfect as action completed but having bearing up the present sometimes necessitates using the English passive in translation.

3. θοῦ δ᾽ ἐν φρενὸς δέλτοισι τοὺς ἐμοὺς λόγους. (Sophocles, *Fragments*)
Put my words in the tablets of the mind.
Put my words on the tablets of your mind.

4. ἡ δὲ τὰ σφυρὰ τοῦ παιδὸς θεραπεύσασα, Οἰδίπουν αὐτὸν καλεῖ τοῦτο θεμένη τὸ ὄνομα διὰ τὸ τοὺς πόδας ἀνοιδῆσαι. (Zenobius, *Proverbs*)

And she, having nursed the ankles of the child, calls him Oedipus, having given this name on account of his feet being swollen.

And she, having nursed the ankles of the child, called him Oedipus, giving him this name on account of his feet being swollen.

- The present is often used in narration of past events.
- τὸ τοὺς πόδας ἀνοιδῆσαι is an articular infinitive.

5. ἐς γῆν δ᾽ Ἀτρεῖδαι πᾶς στρατός τ᾽ ἔστη βλέπων. (Euripides, *Iphigenia in Aulis*)

The Atreidae and all the army stood looking into the ground.

The Atreidae and the whole army stood and stared into the ground.

6. ἀνὰ δ᾽ ὁ πτολίπορθος Ὀδυσσεὺς ἔστη σκῆπτρον ἔχων. (Homer, *Iliad*)

And the city-destroying Odysseus stood holding the scepter.

And up stood Odysseus, the city-destroyer, holding the scepter.

7. καὶ νῦν προσελθὼν στῆθι πλησίον πατρός, σκέψαι δ᾽ ὁποίας συμφορὰς πέπονθα. (Sophocles, *Women of Trachis*)

And now approaching, stand near your father, and look at what sort of misfortunes I have suffered.

And now approach and stand near your father, and behold the misfortunes which I have experienced.

- The use of the circumstantial participle with an imperative sounds awkward in English and is usually best translated as two imperatives.

8. ἐρωτηθεὶς "τί δύσκολον," ἔφη, "τὸ ἑαυτὸν γνῶναι." "τί δὲ εὔκολον," "τὸ ἄλλῳ ὑποθέσθαι." (Thales, in Diogenes Laertius, *Lives of Eminent Philosophers*)

Having been asked "What is hard?" he said, "to know oneself," and to "what is easy?" he said, "to give advice to another."

9. τοίνυν ἀπόδοτε τὰ Καίσαρος Καίσαρι καὶ τὰ τοῦ θεοῦ τῷ θεῷ. (Luke 20:25)

Therefore, return the things of Caesar to Caesar and return the things of God to God.

Accordingly, render unto Caesar what belongs to Caesar, and unto God what belongs to God.

- "Give" is a poor translation of ἀπόδοτε, since it obscures the fact that the admonition is to give something that is already the possession of another.

10   πάτερ ἡμῶν ὁ ἐν τοῖς οὐρανοῖς, ἁγιασθήτω τὸ ὄνομά σου, ἐλθέτω ἡ βασιλεία σου, γενηθήτω τὸ θέλημά σου, ὡς ἐν οὐρανῷ καὶ ἐπὶ γῆς. τὸν ἄρτον ἡμῶν τὸν ἐπιούσιον δὸς ἡμῖν σήμερον·καὶ ἄφες ἡμῖν τὰ ὀφειλήματα ἡμῶν, ὡς καὶ ἡμεῖς ἀφήκαμεν τοῖς ὀφειλέταις ἡμῶν·καὶ μὴ εἰσενέγκῃς ἡμᾶς εἰς πειρασμόν, ἀλλὰ ῥῦσαι ἡμᾶς ἀπὸ τοῦ πονηροῦ. (Matthew 6: 9–13)

- The following translation will be very literal and sound awkward. You can consult the many fine translations available. Since there is disagreement about the translations of certain words like ἐπιούσιον and πονηροῦ, I will include the alternate translations in parentheses.

Our Father, the one in the heavens, let your name be treated as holy, let your kingdom come, let your will come to be, in heaven as on earth. Give us today our daily (supersubstantial) bread, and forgive us our debts (sins), as we have forgiven our debtors. Do not lead us into the trial (temptation), but deliver us from evil (the evil one).

Supplementary Exercises

Write the forms of your three model μι verbs for the following. For ἵστημι, use the 2nd aorist forms.

	δίδωμι	τίθημι	ἵστημι
1st pers., sg., aorist, act., ind.	ἔδωκα	ἔθηκα	ἔστην
2nd pers., sg., aorist, act., imp.	δός	θές	στῆθι
3rd pers., sg., aorist, middle, ind.	ἔδοτο	ἔθετο	NA
1st pers., pl., aorist, middle, ind.	ἐδόμεθα	ἐθέμεθα	NA
aorist active infinitive	δοῦναι	θεῖναι	στῆναι
aorist middle infinitive	δόσθαι	θέσθαι	NA

Identify the gender, number, case, tense, and voice of the following participles.

	Gender	Number	Case	Tense	Voice
δούς	masculine	singular	nominative	aorist	active
δομένην	feminine	singular	accusative	aorist	middle
θεῖσα	feminine	singular	nominative	aorist	active
θέν	neuter	singular	nominative	aorist	active
	neuter	singular	accusative	aorist	active
στάν	neuter	singular	nominative	aorist	active
	neuter	singular	accusative	aorist	active

Translate the following sentences into Greek.
διδάσκαλος, –ου, ὁ = teacher | δίδωμι, δώσω, ἔδωκα, δέδωκα, δέδομαι, ἐδόθην = to give | ἵστημι, στήσω, ἔστησα/ἔστην, ἕστηκα, ἕσταμαι, ἐστάθην = to set; stand

1. The army released the evil men.
ὁ στρατὸς ἀφῆκε τοὺς κακοὺς ἀνθρώπους.

2. The child gave advice to the teacher.
ὁ παῖς ὑπέθετο τῷ διδασκάλῳ.

3. We will suffer the given misfortunes.
πεισόμεθα τὰς δοθέντας συμφοράς.

4. The child stood.
ὁ παῖς ἔστη.

5. The heart suffered many misfortunes.
ἡ φρὴν ἔπαθε πολλὰς συμφοράς.

6. Give (plural) misfortune to the teachers.
δότε τὴν συμφορὴν τοῖς διδασκάλοις. (aorist aspect, so the speaker is thinking of one action)
δίδοτε τὴν συμφορὴν τοῖς διδασκάλοις. (imperfect aspect, so the speaker is thinking of the command as a general rule)

Chapter 32 ⌒

1. νῦν μαχώμεθα φαίδιμ' Ἀχιλλεῦ. (Homer, *Iliad*)
Now let us fight, splendid Achilles.
Now let us fight, famous Achilles.

2. διέλθωμεν δὴ ἕως Βηθλέεμ καὶ ἴδωμεν τὸ ῥῆμα τοῦτο τὸ γεγονὸς ὃ ὁ κύριος
ἐγνώρισεν ἡμῖν. (Luke 2:15)
Let us go unto Bethlehem and let us see this saying, this thing that has
happened which the Lord made known to us.
Let us go to Bethlehem and see this thing which has happened which the
Lord has made know to us.
  - It is difficult to literally translate ῥῆμα here. The shepherds are
    responding to the report that the angels have just given them about
    the birth of Jesus.

3. ἡμεῖς ἀγαπῶμεν, ὅτι αὐτὸς πρῶτος ἠγάπησεν ἡμᾶς. (1 John 4:19)
We love, because he first loved us.
Let us love, since he first loved us.
  - Because alpha contract verb forms are identical in the indicative
    and subjunctive moods, either translation could be correct. Most
    commentators believe the context supports the indicative.

4. ὑπὲρ σεαυτοῦ μὴ φράσῃς ἐγκώμιον. (Menander, *Fragments*)
Do not speak an encomium on behalf of yourself.
Do not give an encomium on behalf of yourself.

5. ἴωμεν καὶ ἀκούσωμεν τοῦ ἀνδρός. (Socrates, in Plato, *Protagoras*)
Let us go and let us hear the man.
Let us go and hear the man.

6. καὶ μὴ εἰσενέγκῃς ἡμᾶς εἰς πειρασμόν. (Luke 11:4)
And do not lead us into the trial.
And lead us not into temptation.

7. ἃ ψέγομεν ἡμεῖς, ταῦτα μὴ μιμώμεθα. (Menander, *Fragments*)
What we criticize, let us not imitate these things.
Let us not imitate the things which we reproach.

8. κύριε, μὴ τῷ θυμῷ σου ἐλέγξῃς με μηδὲ τῇ ὀργῇ σου παιδεύσῃς με. ἐλέησόν με, κύριε, ὅτι ἀσθενής εἰμι. (Psalms 6:1)
Lord, do not test me in your wrath nor teach me in your anger. Have mercy on me, Lord, because I am weak.

9. πάλιν λέγω, μή τίς με δόξῃ ἄφρονα εἶναι. (2 Cor 11:16)
Again, I say, let no one deem me to be senseless.
Again, I say, let no one think that I am a fool.
Again, I say, let no one think that I am foolish.

10. καὶ ἐπηρώτων αὐτὸν οἱ ὄχλοι λέγοντες, "Τί οὖν ποιήσωμεν;" ἀποκριθεὶς δὲ ἔλεγεν αὐτοῖς, "Ὁ ἔχων δύο χιτῶνας μεταδότω τῷ μὴ ἔχοντι, καὶ ὁ ἔχων βρώματα ὁμοίως ποιείτω." (Luke 3:10–11)
And the crowd was questioning him, saying "What shall we do?", and answering he said to them "The one having two cloaks, let him give to the one not having, and the one having food, let him do likewise."

And the crowd questioned him and said to him, "What shall we do?". And he answered and said to them "The one having two cloaks, let him give one of them to the one not having any, and the one having food, let him do likewise."

And the crowd questioned him and said to him, "What shall we do?". And he answered and said to them "The one who has two cloaks, let him give one of them to the one who does not have one, and the one who has food, let him do likewise."

Supplementary Exercises

Give the corresponding subjunctive forms for the following indicative forms.

εἰμί	ὦ	δηλοῦμεν	δηλῶμεν
ἐστί	ᾖ	δίδωσιν	διδῷ
λύω	λύω	δίδοται	διδῶται
λύεται	λύηται	ἔδωκα	δῷ
λύονται	λύωνται	τίθεσθε	τιθῆσθε
νικῶ	νικῶ	τίθενται	τιθῶνται
νικᾷς	νικᾷς	τιθέασιν	τιθῇ
φιλεῖς	φιλῇς	ἵσταμεν	ἱστῶμεν
ἐφίλησαν	φιλήσωσιν	ἔστη	στῇ
δηλοῖ	δηλοῖ	ἵστημι	ἱστῶ

Translate the following sentences into Greek.
διδάσκαλος, –ου, ὁ = teacher

1. Let us fight the senseless crowd.
μαχώμεθα τὸν ἄφρονα ὄχλον.

2. Don't (singular) criticize the weak. (Don't use an imperative.)
μή ψέγῃς τοὺς ἀσθενεῖς.
   - A present subjunctive is used here rather than an aorist subjunctive, as it is a general prohibition. The aorist subjunctive does, however, occasionally show up in such constructions.

3. Let us not think that the weak are senseless.
μὴ δοξάζωμεν τοὺς ἀσθενεῖς εἶναι ἄφρονας.

4. Shall we declare that an encomium is senseless?

φράζωμεν ὅτι τὸ ἐγκώμιόν ἐστιν ἄφρον·

φράζωμεν τὸ ἐγκώμιον εἶναι ἄφρον;

5. Shall I criticize the senseless teacher? (Don't use a future.)

ψέγω τὸν ἄφρονα διδάσκαλον;

Since the present subjunctive and present indicative of ψέγω are identical, context would determine whether this was a statement of fact or a deliberative subjunctive.

6. Let us not imitate the senseless teacher.

μὴ μιμώμεθα τὸν ἄφρονα διδάσκαλον.

Chapter 33 ~

1. τούτου χάριν πάντα πράττομεν, ὅπως μήτε ἀλγῶμεν μήτε ταρβῶμεν. (Epicurus, *Letter to Menoeceus*)

For the sake of this we do all things, so that we neither suffer nor be afraid.
For the sake of the following do we do everything: lest we suffer or be afraid.

- "Lest" works really well for negative purpose clauses, but if it sounds too odd for you, use "so that not" or "in order to not."

2. πᾶς γὰρ ὁ φαῦλα πράσσων μισεῖ τὸ φῶς καὶ οὐκ ἔρχεται πρὸς τὸ φῶς, ἵνα μὴ ἐλεγχθῇ τὰ ἔργα αὐτοῦ. (John 3:20)

For everyone doing base things hates the light and does not come to the light, lest their works be tested.
For everyone doing wicked things hates the light and does not come to the light, in order that their works not be exposed.

3. οὐ γὰρ ἦλθον ἵνα κρίνω τὸν κόσμον ἀλλ᾽ ἵνα σώσω τὸν κόσμον. (John 12:47)

For I did not come in order to condemn the world, but in order to save the world.
For I did not come to condemn the world, but to save it.

4. μὴ κρίνετε, ἵνα μὴ κριθῆτε. (Matthew 7:1)
Do not condemn, lest you be condemned.
Do not judge, so that you are not judged.

- The use of the present imperative κρίνετε with the aorist passive imperative κριθῆτε suggests that the translation "condemn" is more accurate than "judge."

5. διὰ τοῦτο δύο ὦτα ἔχομεν, στόμα δὲ ἕν, ἵνα πλείονα μὲν ἀκούωμεν, ἥττονα δὲ λέγωμεν. (Zeno of Citium, in Diogenes Laertius, *Lives of Eminent Philosophers*)

On account of this we have two ears and one mouth, so that we hear more things and speak less things.

For this reason we have two ears but one mouth, so that we listen more and speak less.

6. μὴ σπεῦδε πλουτεῖν, μὴ ταχὺς πένης γένῃ. (Menander, *Fragments*)

Do not hasten to be wealthy, lest you quickly become poor.

- As we have seen, Greek often prefers an adjective where English prefers an adverb, hence the translation of the adjective "quick" as "quickly."

7. κἀγὼ τὴν δόξαν ἣν δέδωκάς μοι δέδωκα αὐτοῖς, ἵνα ὦσιν ἓν καθὼς ἡμεῖς ἕν. (John 17:22)

And the glory which you have given to me, I have given to them, so that they may be one just as we are one.

8. σύ τ᾽, Ἰνάχειον σπέρμα, τοὺς ἐμοὺς λόγους θυμῷ βάλ᾽, ὡς τέρματ᾽ ἐκμάθῃς ὁδοῦ. (Aeschylus, *Prometheus Bound*)

And you, Inachean seed, put my words in your spirit, so that you may learn the end of the road.

And you, daughter of Inachus, put my words in your heart, so that you learn the end of your journey.

9. ὁ Σωκράτης δ᾽ ἔλεγεν τῶν ἄλλων ἀνθρώπων διαφέρειν καθ᾽ ὅσον οἱ μὲν ζῶσιν ἵν᾽ ἐσθίωσιν, αὐτὸς δ᾽ ἐσθίει ἵνα ζῇ. (Athenaeus, *Deinosophistae*)

And Socrates used to say that he differed from other people in as much as they lived in order to eat, but he ate in order to live.

- Remember that when the subject of the indirect statement in accusative + infinitive is also the subject of the verb that introduces the indirect statement, the subject, here Socrates, need not be repeated.

10. καὶ ἀποκριθεὶς ὁ Ἰησοῦς εἶπεν πρὸς αὐτούς, "Οὐ χρείαν ἔχουσιν οἱ ὑγιαίνοντες ἰατροῦ ἀλλὰ οἱ κακῶς ἔχοντες. οὐκ ἐλήλυθα καλέσαι δικαίους ἀλλὰ ἁμαρτωλοὺς εἰς μετάνοιαν." (Luke 5:31–32)
And Jesus, answering said to them, "Those being healthy do not have need of a physician, but those faring poorly. I have not come to call the just, but sinners to repentance."
And Jesus answered them and said, "The healthy do not need a doctor, but the sick do. I have come to call sinners, not the just, to repentance.

Supplementary Exercises

Translate the following sentences into Greek. γίγνομαι (Koine γίνομαι), γενήσομαι, ἐγενόμην, γέγονα, γεγένημαι, — = to become | διδάσκαλος, -ου, ὁ = teacher | διδάσκω, διδάξω, ἐδίδαξα, δεδίδαχα, δεδίδαγμαι, ἐδιδάχθην = to teach | εἰμί = to be | εὐδαίμων, -ον (adj.) = happy | ἤ (conj.) = or; than | Σωκράτης, -ους, ὁ = Socrates.

1. I am not teaching in order to become rich.
οὐ διδάσκω ἵνα γένωμαι πλούσιος.
- The aorist subjunctive is more common than the present subjunctive.
οὐ διδάσκω ὅπως γένωμαι πλούσιος.
οὐ διδάσκω ὡς γένωμαι πλούσιος.
οὐ διδάσκω ἵνα γένωμαι πλούσια. (If the speaker is female)

2. Socrates was poor so that he could be happy.
ὁ Σωκράτης ἦν πένης ἵνα ᾖ εὐδαίμων.

3. Let the teachers not teach in order to condemn.
οἱ διδάσκαλοι μὴ διδασκόντων ἵνα κρίνωσιν.

4. Socrates will not teach to become rich.
ὁ Σωκράτης οὐ διδάξει ἵνα ᾖ πλούσιος.

5. Let us strive to be more than mouths.

σπευδῶμεν ἵνα ὦμεν πλείονες ἢ στόματα.

σπευδῶμεν εἶναι πλείονες ἢ στόματα.

- Even in an accusative and infinitive construction, if the subject is the same as the finite verb, the nominative is retained if the subject is modified by an adjective. Hence πλείονες, not πλείονας, in the second example.

Chapter 34 ～

1. ὦ δύσποτμ᾽, εἴθε μήποτε γνοίης ὃς εἶ. (Sophocles, *Oedipus Tyrannus*)
Oh misfortunate one, may you never know who you are.
Oh wretched one, I wish that you never learn who you are.

2. ἀστέρας εἰσαθρεῖς, ἀστὴρ ἐμός· εἴθε γενοίμην
οὐρανός, ὡς πολλοῖσ᾽ ὄμμασιν εἰς σὲ βλέπω.
(Plato, *Epigrams*)
You look upon the stars, my star. May I turn into the sky, to see you with many eyes.
My star, you gaze upon the stars. May I turn into the sky, that I be able to look at you with many eyes.

3. εἶπεν δὲ Μαριάμ, "Ἰδοὺ ἡ δούλη κυρίου· γένοιτό μοι κατὰ τὸ ῥῆμά σου."
καὶ ἀπῆλθεν ἀπ᾽ αὐτῆς ὁ ἄγγελος. (Luke 1:38)
And Mary said, "Behold, the servant of the Lord. May it happen to me according to your word."
And Mary said, "Look. I am the servant of the Lord. May it happen to me as you say."

4. εἰ ἄρα ὁ Ἔρως τῶν καλῶν ἐνδεής ἐστι, τὰ δὲ ἀγαθὰ καλά, κἂν τῶν ἀγαθῶν
ἐνδεὴς εἴη. (Plato, *Symposium*)
If then Eros is lacking of beautiful things, and good things are beautiful, Eros would also lack good things.
If then Love lacks beauty, and the good is the beautiful, he would also lack the good.

5. μή μοι γένοιθ᾽, ἃ βούλομ᾽, ἀλλ᾽ ἃ συμφέρει. (Menander, *Fragments*)

May what I want not happen to me, but what is beneficial.

6. τί οὖν ἐροῦμεν; ἐπιμένωμεν τῇ ἁμαρτίᾳ ἵνα ἡ χάρις πλεονάσῃ; μὴ γένοιτο·
οἵτινες ἀπεθάνομεν τῇ ἁμαρτίᾳ, πῶς ἔτι ζήσομεν ἐν αὐτῇ; (Rom 6:1–2)

What then shall we say? Shall we remain in sin in order that grace increase?
May it not be! We who have died to sin, how will we still live in it?

7. σοῦ γὰρ φθιμένης οὐκέτ᾽ ἂν εἴην. (Euripides, *Alcestis*)

For, if you should perish, I would no longer exist.

For, if you die, I would no longer exist.

For if you die, I could no longer exist.

8. μανείην μᾶλλον ἢ ἡσθείην. (Antisthenes, in Diogenes Laertius, *Lives
of Eminent Philosophers)*

May I be crazy rather than feel pleasure.

I would rather lose my mind than feel pleasure.

9. φεῦ φεῦ, βροτείων πημάτων ὅσαι τύχαι
ὅσαι τε μορφαί· τέρμα δ᾽ οὐκ εἴποι τις ἄν.
(Euripides, *Antiope*)

Alas, alas. How many are the fortunes of mortals and how many the
forms. One could not say the limit.

Alas, alas. How numerous are the fortunes and forms of mortals. One
could not name their end.

10. χάρις ὑμῖν καὶ εἰρήνη πληθυνθείη ἐν ἐπιγνώσει τοῦ θεοῦ καὶ Ἰησοῦ τοῦ
κυρίου ἡμῶν. (2 Peter 1:2)

Grace to you and may peace be multiplied in the knowledge of God and
Jesus our Lord.

May grace and peace be multiplied for you in the knowledge of God and
Jesus our Lord.

- Both translations are grammatically correct; it depends on whether
  χάρις is taken on its own with ὑμῖν or together with εἰρήνη
  πληθυνθείη.

Supplementary Exercises

Give the corresponding optative forms for the following indicative forms.

εἰμί	εἴην	δηλοῦμεν	δηλοῖμεν
ἐστί	εἴη	δίδωσιν	διδοῖεν
λύω	λύοιμι	δίδοται	διδοῖτο
λύσεται	λύσοιτο	ἔδωκα	δοίη
λύονται	λύοιντο	τίθεσθε	τιθεῖσθε
νικῶ	νικῴην	τίθενται	τιθεῖντο
νικᾷς	νικῴης	τιθέασιν	τιθεῖεν
φιλεῖς	φιλοίης	ἵσταμεν	ἱσταῖμεν
ἐφίλησαν	φιλήσειαν	στήσω	στήσοιμι

Translate the following sentences into Greek.
❡ εἰμί = to be | Σωκράτης, –ους, ὁ = Socrates |
εὐδαίμων, –ον (adj.) = happy

1. Adversity could benefit the happy.
ἡ πῆμα συμφέροι ἂν τοὺς εὐδαίμονας.

2. How could the forms of misfortune still increase?
πῶς αἱ μορφαὶ τῶν πημάτων ἔτι πλεονάσειαν ἄν;

3. May the recognition of adversity be useful. (Use an optative.)
ἡ ἐπίγνωσις τοῦ πήματος συμφέροι.

4. Socrates might be crazy.
ὁ Σωκράτης μαίνοιτο ἄν.

5. I wish that I were happy.
εἴην εὐδαίμων.
The speaker here thinks that happiness is a possibility. Impossible wishes are covered in chapter 37.

Chapter 35 ～

1. ἡμεῖς γὰρ ὁπότ᾿ ἀρχόμεθα ζῆν, τότ᾿ ἀποθνήσκομεν. (Theophrastus, Diogenes Laertius, *Lives of Eminent Philosophers*)

For whenever we begin to live, then we die.

For when we begin to live, at that point we die.

- Simple condition

2. ἤγαγεν δὲ αὐτὸν εἰς Ἰερουσαλὴμ καὶ ἔστησεν ἐπὶ τὸ πτερύγιον τοῦ ἱεροῦ, καὶ εἶπεν αὐτῷ, "Εἰ υἱὸς εἶ τοῦ θεοῦ, βάλε σεαυτὸν ἐντεῦθεν κάτω. (Luke 4:9)

He led him to Jerusalem and stood him on the turret of the temple, and he said to him, "If you are the son of God, throw yourself down from here."

- Mixed condition with an imperative in place of the apodosis.

3. ἐὰν δ᾿ ἔχωμεν χρήμαθ᾿, ἕξομεν φίλους. (Menander, *Fragments*)

If we have money, we will have friends.

- Future more vivid condition

4. ἐγώ εἰμι ὁ ἄρτος ὁ ζῶν ὁ ἐκ τοῦ οὐρανοῦ καταβάς· ἐάν τις φάγῃ ἐκ τούτου τοῦ ἄρτου ζήσει εἰς τὸν αἰῶνα. (John 6:51)

I am the bread, the living bread having come down from heaven. If someone eats from this bread, he will live forever.

I am the living bread that has come down from heaven. If someone shall eat from this bread, he will live forever.

I am the living break that has descended from heaven, whoever eats of it shall live forever.

- Future more vivid condition

5. ἄν τι αἰτήσητε τὸν πατέρα ἐν τῷ ὀνόματί μου δώσει ὑμῖν. (John 16:23)

If you ask for the Father for something in my name, he will give it to you.

Whatever you ask the Father for in my name, he will give it to you.

- ἄν = ἐάν
- Future more vivid condition

6. ὃς γὰρ ἂν θέλῃ τὴν ψυχὴν αὐτοῦ σῶσαι, ἀπολέσει αὐτήν· ὃς δ᾽ ἂν ἀπολέσῃ τὴν ψυχὴν αὐτοῦ ἕνεκεν ἐμοῦ, οὗτος σώσει αὐτήν. (Luke 9:24)

For he who wishes to save his life will lose it. And he who loses his life for my sake, this one will save it.

For whoever wishes to save his life will lose it, and whoever loses his life for my sake, he will save it.

For whoever wishes to save his life will lose it, and whoever loses his life for my sake will save it.

- Future more vivid condition with a relative pronoun in place of εἰ.

7. κακοῖς ὁμιλῶν καὐτὸς ἐκβήσῃ κακός. (Menander, *Fragments*)

Living with evil men, you will also turn out evil.

If you live with evil people, you will also turn out evil.

If you live with evil people, even you will turn out evil.

- Most likely a conditional participle, but you could also make a case for a temporal or causal circumstantial participle, i.e. "When you live with evil people…" or "Since you live with evil people…" This is another reason why it is often best to translate participles literally.

8. οὐκ ἔστιν οὐδείς, ὅστις οὐχ αὑτῷ φίλος. (Menander, *Fragments*)

There is no one who is not friendly to himself.

There is no one who is not a friend to himself.

There does not exist anyone who is not a friend to himself.

- Pay attention to the breathing of αὑτῷ, which makes this a reflexive pronoun. αὐτῷ would make this a 3rd person personal pronoun.

9. ἀλλ' οὐ τὰ θεῖα κρυπτόντων θεῶν μάθοις ἄν, οὐδ' εἰ πάντ' ἐπεξέλθοις
σκοπῶν. (Sophocles, *Fragments*)
But you would not learn the divine things of the hidden gods, not even
if, going out, you should look at everything.
But you would not learn the sacred things of the hidden gods, not even if
you should go out and examine everything.
* Future less vivid condition

10. μᾶλλον ἄν τὰ πολιτικὰ πράττοιμι, εἰ μόνος αὐτὰ πράττοιμι. (Socrates, in
Xenophon, *Memorabilia*)
I would do politics more if I could do them alone.
* Future less vivid condition

Supplementary Exercises

εἰ γὰρ ἕξομεν τὴν ταπεινοφροσύνην, ἕξομεν τὴν ἀρχὴν τῆς σοφίας.
For if we will have humility, we will have the beginning of wisdom.

1. Change the above simple condition into a future more vivid condition.
ἐὰν γὰρ ἔχωμεν τὴν ταπεινοφροσύνην, ἕξομεν τὴν ἀρχὴν τῆς σοφίας.

2. Change the above simple condition into a future less vivid condition.
εἰ γὰρ ἔχοιμεν τὴν ταπεινοφροσύνην, ἔχοιμεν τὴν ἀρχὴν τῆς σοφίας ἄν.

3. Replace the protasis of the above simple condition with a conditional
participle.
ἔχοντες τὴν ταπεινοφροσύνην, ἕξομεν τὴν ἀρχὴν τῆς σοφίας.

4. Replace εἰ of the above simple condition with a relative pronoun. Be
sure to change the person of the verb as well.
οἵτινες γὰρ ἕξουσι τὴν ταπεινοφροσύνην, ἕξουσι τὴν ἀρχὴν τῆς σοφίας.

Translate the following sentences into Greek.
εἰμί = to be | Σωκράτης, -ους, ὁ = Socrates |
εὐδαίμων, -ον (adj.) = happy

1. If we destroy the temple, we will destroy the holy things.

ἐὰν ἀπολέσωμεν τὸ ἱερὸν, ἀπολοῦμεν τὰ ἱερά.

- future more vivid
- The aorist subjunctive is more common that the present subjunctive ἀπολλύωμεν.
- Remember that the future tense of ἀπόλλυμι is a liquid future.

2. If we should destroy the temple, we would destroy the holy things.

εἰ ἀπολέσαιμεν τὸ ἱερὸν, ἀπολέσαιμεν τὰ ἱερὰ ἄν.

- future less vivid, aorist optatives

3. If I destroy the political things, Socrates will be happy.

ἐὰν ἀπολέσω τὰ πολιτικὰ, ὁ Σωκράτης ἔσται εὐδαίμων.

- future more vivid, aorist subjunctive

4. If I should destroy the political things, Socrates would be happy.

εἰ ἀπολέσαιμι τὰ πολιτικὰ, ὁ Σωκράτης εἴη εὐδαίμων ἄν.

- future less vivid, aorist optatives

5. Whoever destroys the temple will destroy the holy things.

ὅστις ἂν ἀπολέσῃ τὸ ἱερὸν, ἀπολεῖ τὰ ἱερά.

- equivalent of a future more vivid condition.
- Remember that ἀπόλλυμι is a liquid future.

6. When you (singular) destroy the temple, you destroy the holy things.

ὅταν ἀπολέσῃς τὸ ἱερὸν, ἀπόλλυς τὰ ἱερά.

- ἀπόλλυς, a μι verb, is classical, but you will see later uses of ἀπολλύεις, as if it were an omega verb.
- present general

7. When you (singular) destroy the temple, don't destroy the holy things.

ὅταν ἀπολέσῃς τὸ ἱερὸν, μὴ ἀπολέσῃς τὰ ἱερά.

- mixed condition, prohibitive subjunctive.

ὅταν ἀπολέσῃς τὸ ἱερὸν, μὴ ἀπόλλυε τὰ ἱερά.

- mixed condition, imperative

Chapter 36 ～

1. ἀνὴρ πονηρὸς δυστυχεῖ, κἂν εὐτυχῇ. (Menander, *Fragments*)
A wicked man is unfortunate, even if he is fortunate.
An evil man is unhappy, even if he is happy.
   • Present general condition

2. ἀμὴν ἀμὴν λέγω ὑμῖν, ἐὰν μὴ ὁ κόκκος τοῦ σίτου πεσὼν εἰς τὴν γῆν ἀποθάνῃ, αὐτὸς μόνος μένει· ἐὰν δὲ ἀποθάνῃ, πολὺν καρπὸν φέρει. (John 12:24)
Amen, amen I say to you, if a grain of wheat does not die, having fallen upon the ground, it alone remains. But if it dies, it bears much fruit.
Truly, truly I say to you, unless a grain of wheat falls upon the ground and dies, it alone remains. But if it dies, it bears much fruit.
   • Present general condition

3. λέγει ἡ μήτηρ αὐτοῦ τοῖς διακόνοις, "Ὅ τι ἂν λέγῃ ὑμῖν ποιήσατε." (John 2:5)
His mother says to the servants, "Whatever he says to you, do it."
His mother says to the servants, "Do whatever he says to you."
   • A mixed condition that starts as a present general or future more vivid (they have the same protasis), but then has an imperative in the apodosis.

4. ἀλλ' εἴ τι μὴ φέροιμεν ὤτρυνεν φέρειν. (Euripides, *Alcestis*)
But if we did not bring something, he ordered us to bring it.
   • Past general condition

5. τὸ φρικωδέστατον οὖν τῶν κακῶν ὁ θάνατος οὐδὲν πρὸς ἡμᾶς, ὅταν περ μὲν ἡμεῖς ὦμεν, ὁ θάνατος οὐ πάρεστιν. (Epicurus, in Diogenes Laertius, *Lives of Eminent Philosophers*)

Therefore, the most horrible of evils, death, is nothing to us. For whenever we exist, death is not present."

- Present general condition

6. εἴ ποτε βουλεύσαιμι φίλῳ κακόν, αὐτὸς ἔχοιμι. (Theognis, *Elegies*)

If I should ever wish evil upon a friend, may I myself have it (the evil.)

- This mixed condition begins as a future less vivid condition, but instead of the optative + ἄν in the apodosis, we have an optative of wish. The presence, of lack thereof, of one little word, ἄν, makes a big difference in the meaning.

7. διὸ εὐδοκῶ ἐν ἀσθενείαις, ἐν ὕβρεσιν, ἐν ἀνάγκαις, ἐν διωγμοῖς καὶ στενοχωρίαις, ὑπὲρ Χριστοῦ· ὅταν γὰρ ἀσθενῶ, τότε δυνατός εἰμι. (2 Cor 12:10)

On account of this I am pleased with weaknesses, insults, necessities, persecutions, and difficulties on behalf of Christ. For whenever I am weak, then I am strong.

- Present general condition

8. καὶ ὅταν τις ἐξίῃ τῆς οἰκίας, ζητείτω πρότερον τί μέλλει πράσσειν καὶ ὅταν εἰσέλθῃ πάλιν, ζητείτω τί ἔπραξε. (Cleobulus, in Diogenes Laertius, *Lives of Eminent Philosophers*)

Whenever one exits the house, let him first seek what he is about to do. And whenever he returns again, let him seek what he did.

Whenever one exits the house, let him first ask what he is about to do. And whenever he returns again, let him ask what he did.

- Mixed conditions

9. ὃς ἂν δέξηται τοῦτο τὸ παιδίον ἐπὶ τῷ ὀνόματί μου ἐμὲ δέχεται, καὶ ὃς ἂν ἐμὲ δέξηται δέχεται τὸν ἀποστείλαντά με. (Luke 9:48)

He who receives this child in my name receives me, and he who receives me receives the one having sent me.

Whoever receives this child in my name receives me, and whoever receives me receives the one who sent me.

- Present general conditions

10. τότε γὰρ ἡδονῆς χρείαν ἔχομεν ὅταν ἐκ τοῦ μὴ παρεῖναι τὴν ἡδονὴν ἀλγῶμεν· ὅταν δὲ μὴ ἀλγῶμεν, οὐκέτι τῆς ἡδονῆς δεόμεθα. καὶ διὰ τοῦτο τὴν ἡδονὴν ἀρχὴν καὶ τέλος λέγομεν εἶναι τοῦ μακαρίως ζῆν. (Epicurus, *Letter to Menoeceus*)

For then we have need of pleasure, whenever we suffer from pleasure not being present. And whenever we do not suffer, we no longer need pleasure. And on account of this we say that pleasure is the beginning and end of living happily.

For whenever we suffer from pleasure not being present, then we need pleasure. And whenever we do not suffer, we no longer need pleasure. And on account of this we say that pleasure is the beginning and the end of a happy life.

Supplementary Exercises

εἰ γὰρ ἕξομεν τὴν ταπεινοφροσύνην, ἕξομεν τὴν ἀρχὴν τῆς σοφίας.
For if we will have humility, we will have the beginning of wisdom.

1. Change the above simple condition into a present general condition.
ἐὰν γὰρ ἔχωμεν τὴν ταπεινοφροσύνην, ἔχομεν τὴν ἀρχὴν τῆς σοφίας.
ἤν and /ἄν could be used instead of ἐάν

2. Change the above simple condition into a present general condition with ὅταν.
ὅταν γὰρ ἔχωμεν τὴν ταπεινοφροσύνην, ἔχομεν τὴν ἀρχὴν τῆς σοφίας.

3. Change the above simple condition into a past general condition.
εἰ γὰρ ἔχοιμεν τὴν ταπεινοφροσύνην, εἴχομεν τὴν ἀρχὴν τῆς σοφίας.

4. Change the above simple condition into a present general condition with a conditional participle.
ἔχοντες τὴν ταπεινοφροσύνην, ἔχομεν τὴν ἀρχὴν τῆς σοφίας.

Fill in the following flowcharts.

Protasis (if clause) ἐάν (ἤν, ἄν) + Subjunctive	Apodosis (then clause) Future Indicative	Future More Vivid
	Apodosis (then clause) Present Indicative	Present General
Protasis (if clause) εἰ + Optative	Apodosis (then clause) Optative + ἄν	Future Less Vivid
	Apodosis (then clause) Imperfect Indicative	Past General

Translate the following sentences into Greek.

εἰμί = to be | καλέω, καλῶ, ἐκάλεσα, κέκληκα, κέκλημαι, ἐκλήθην = to call | Σωκράτης, –ους, ὁ = Socrates

1. When necessity is present, the servant is present.
ὅταν ἡ ἀνάγκη παρῇ, ὁ διάκονος πάρεστιν.

2. When necessity was present, Socrates was present.
εἰ ἡ ἀνάγκη παρείη, ὁ Σωκράτης παρῆν.

3. Whenever the servant is weak, there is no bread.
ὅταν ὁ διάκονος ἀσθενῶ, οὐκ ἔστιν ὁ σίτος.

4. Call (plural) us whenever Socrates is weak.
καλεῖτε ἡμᾶς ὅταν ὁ Σωκράτης ἀσθενῇ.

5. If Socrates was ever weak, we were present.
εἰ ὁ Σωκράτης ἀσθενοίη, παρῆμεν.

Chapter 37 ～

1. εἰ γὰρ ἐπιστεύετε Μωϋσεῖ, ἐπιστεύετε ἂν ἐμοί, περὶ γὰρ ἐμοῦ ἐκεῖνος ἔγραψεν. (John 5:46)

For if you trusted Moses, you would trust me. For that one wrote about me.

For if you had faith in Moses, you would have faith in me. For he wrote about me.

For if you believed Moses, you would also believe me. For that one wrote about me.

- Present unreal condition

2. εἰ μὴ γὰρ ὅρκοις θεῶν ἄφαρκτος ἡρέθην, οὐκ ἂν ποτ' ἔσχον μὴ οὐ τάδ' ἐξειπεῖν πατρί. (Euripides, *Hippolytus*)

For if I had not been held defenseless by oaths of the gods, I would not have been able not to speak these things to my father.

- Past unreal condition

3. ἔλεγον οὖν αὐτῷ, "Ποῦ ἐστιν ὁ πατήρ σου;" ἀπεκρίθη Ἰησοῦς, "Οὔτε ἐμὲ οἴδατε οὔτε τὸν πατέρα μου· εἰ ἐμὲ ᾔδειτε, καὶ τὸν πατέρα μου ἂν ᾔδειτε." (John 8:19)

And they were saying to him, "Where is your father?" Jesus answered, "You know neither me nor my father. If you knew me, you would know my father."

- Pluperfects of defective verbs are used here as the equivalent of a present unreal condition.

4. εἶπεν οὖν ἡ Μάρθα πρὸς τὸν Ἰησοῦν, "Κύριε, εἰ ἦς ὧδε οὐκ ἂν ἀπέθανεν ὁ ἀδελφός μου." (John 11:21)
Then Martha said to Jesus, "Lord, if you had been here, my brother would not have died."
- Past unreal condition. Because there is no aorist form of εἰμί, the imperfect (ἦς is a late form of ἦσθα) is used.

5. Orestes: εἴθ' ἦν Ὀρέστης πλησίον κλύων τάδε.
Electra: ἀλλ', ὦ ξέν', οὐ γνοίην ἂν εἰσιδοῦσά νιν.
(Euripides, *Electra*)
Orestes: Would that Orestes were near hearing these things.
Electra: But, oh stranger, seeing him, I would not know him.
Orestes: Would that Orestes were near hearing these things.
Electra: But, oh stranger, I would not recognize him if I saw him.
- The first line contains an unattainable wish. The last line contains a potential optative.

6. ἰὼ Λάϊειον τέκνον, εἴθε σ' εἴθε σε μήποτ' εἶδον. (Sophocles, *Oedipus Tyrannus*)
Alas child of Laius. Would that, oh would that, I had never seen you.
- Unattainable wish

7. οὐ γὰρ ἄν ποτε θνήσκων ἐσώθην, μὴ 'πί τῳ δεινῷ κακῷ. (Sophocles, *Oedipus Tyrannus*)
For dying I would never have been saved if not for some terrible evil.
For I would never have been saved from dying if not for some terrible evil.
- The equivalent of a past unreal condition. The verb in the protasis (μὴ 'πί τῳ δεινῷ κακῷ) is implied.

8. εἴθε γὰρ αἱ κρῆναι καὶ ἄρτους ἔφερον. (Crates, in Diogenes, *Lives of Eminent Philosophers*)
Would that springs also produced bread.
If only springs also bore bread.
- Unattainable wish

9. εἰ γὰρ κατιδεῖν βίου τέλος ἦν. (Theognis, *Elegies*)
Would that it were possible to see the end of life.
If only it were possible to see the end of life.
- Unattainable wish

10. εἰ μὴ πατὴρ ἦσθ᾽, εἶπον ἄν σ᾽ οὐκ εὖ φρονεῖν. (Sophocles, *Antigone*)
If you were not my father, I would have said you were not thinking well.
- Mixed unreal condition

Supplementary Exercises

Translate the following sentences into Greek.
διδάσκαλος, –ου, ὁ = teacher | φυλάττω (Koine φυλάσσω), φυλάξω, ἐφύλαξα, πεφύλαχα, πεφύλαγμαι, ἐφυλάχθην = to guard

1. If the teacher were terrible, I would guard the child.
εἰ ὁ διδάσκαλος ἦν δεινός, ἐφύλαττον ἄν τὸ τέκνον. (classical)
εἰ ὁ διδάσκαλος ἦν δεινός, ἐφύλασσον ἄν τὸ τέκνον. (koine)

2. If I had seen the terrible stranger, I would have seized him.
εἰ εἰσεῖδον τὸν δεινὸν ξένον, εἷλον ἄν αὐτόν.

3. If we were not terrible, we would not be seized here.
εἰ οὐκ ἦμεν δεινοί, ἡρούμεθα ὧδε.

4. If only the oath were not terrible.
εἰ γὰρ ὁ ὅρκος μὴ ἦν δεινός.
εἴθε ὁ ὅρκος μὴ ἦν δεινός.

5. If only I had not seen the terrible things.
εἰ γὰρ μὴ εἰσεῖδον τὰ δεινά.
εἴθε μὴ εἰσεῖδον τὰ δεινά.

Chapter 38 ⟡

1. εἰ μέν τις φοβεῖται μὴ ἀποβάλλῃ τὴν οὐσίαν, οὗτος δειλός, εἰ δέ τις θαρσεῖ περὶ ταῦτα, ἀνδρεῖος; (Aristotle, *Magna Moralia*)

If someone is afraid that they will lose their possessions, is this person cowardly? And if someone is courageous about these things, is he brave? If someone is afraid to lose their possessions, is this person a coward? And if someone is courageous about these things, is he brave?

- Fear clause

2. ὑμεῖς, ὦ Λακεδαιμόνιοι, ἡ μόνη ἐλπίς, δέδιμεν μὴ οὐ βέβαιοι ἦτε. (Thucydides, *History of the Peloponnesian War*)

You, oh Lacedemonians, are our only hope, but we fear that you are not steadfast.

Oh Spartans, you are our only hope, but we are afraid that you are not dependable.

- Fear clause with a subjunctive (action not yet done). See #3 below for a fear clause with an indicative.

3. ἐπαινούμενός ποτε ὑπὸ πονηρῶν, ἔφη, "ἀγωνιῶ μή τι κακὸν εἴργασμαι." (Antisthenes, in Diogenes Laertius, *Lives of Eminent Philosophers*)

Having once been praised by wicked men, he said, "I am afraid that I have done something evil."

When he was once praised by wicked men, he said, "I fear that I have done something evil."

- Fear clause with an indicative (action already completed).

153

4. εἰ δὲ ἀλλήλους δάκνετε καὶ κατεσθίετε, βλέπετε μὴ ὑπ᾽ ἀλλήλων ἀναλωθῆτε. (Gal 5:15)

But if you bite and devour each other, watch out lest you are consumed by each other.

But if you bite and devour one another, take care that you are not consumed by one another.

- Object clause of caution

5. ἀγωνίζεσθε εἰσελθεῖν διὰ τῆς στενῆς θύρας, ὅτι πολλοί, λέγω ὑμῖν, ζητήσουσιν εἰσελθεῖν καὶ οὐκ ἰσχύσουσιν. (Luke 13:24)

Strive to enter through the narrow gate, because many, I say to you, will seek to enter but will not be able to.

Work hard to enter through the narrow gate, because many, I tell you, will seek to enter but will not be able to.

6. ἔλεγε συνετῶν μὲν ἀνδρῶν, πρὶν γενέσθαι τὰ δυσχερῆ, προνοῆσαι ὅπως μὴ γένηται. (Pittacus, in Diogenes Laertius, *Lives of Eminent Philosophers*)

He used to say that it was of intelligent men, before difficult things happen, to see to it that they not happen.

He said that it was the sign of intelligent men to see that difficult things not happen before they occur.

- A rare case of an effort clause taking a subjunctive.

7. ὁ δὲ εἶπεν, " Βλέπετε μὴ πλανηθῆτε· πολλοὶ γὰρ ἐλεύσονται ἐπὶ τῷ ὀνόματί μου λέγοντες, Ἐγώ εἰμι· καί, Ὁ καιρὸς ἤγγικεν· μὴ πορευθῆτε ὀπίσω αὐτῶν." (Luke 21:8)

And he said, "See to it lest you are led astray. For many will come in my name saying, 'I am,' and 'the time has come.' Do not follow after them."

And he said, "See to it that you are not led astray. For many will come in my name saying, 'I am He,' and 'the time has come.' Do not follow after them."

- Object clause of caution

8. ὦ μέγ᾽ εὔδαιμον κόρη, τί παρθενεύῃ δαρόν, ἐξόν σοι γάμου τυχεῖν μεγίστου. (Aeschylus, *Prometheus Bound*)

Oh very happy girl. Why do you remain unmarried so long, it being possible for you to obtain the greatest wedding?

Oh very fortunate maiden. Why do you remain unmarried for so long, when it is possible for you to obtain the greatest wedding bed?

9. τίς εὐδαίμων, "ὃ τὸ μὲν σῶμα ὑγιής, τὴν δὲ ψυχὴν εὔπορος, τὴν δὲ φύσιν εὐπαίδευτος." (Thales, in Diogenes Laertius, *Lives of Eminent Philosophers*)

Who is happy? The one healthy in body, resourceful in life, and by nature quick to learn.

Who is the happy man? The one healthy in body, resourceful in spirit, and by nature quick to learn.

10. τυφλὸς τά τ᾽ ὦτα τόν τε νοῦν τά τ᾽ ὄμματ᾽ εἶ. (Sophocles, *Oedipus Tyrannus*)

You are blind in your ears and in your mind and in your eyes.

You are blind in ears, mind, and eyes.

Supplementary Exercises

Fill in the following charts.

Main Verb	Fear Clause	
The subject fears that something will happen.	verb of fearing	μή + subjunctive
The subject fears that something will not happen.	verb of fearing	μὴ οὐ + subjunctive
The subject fears that something has happened or is happening.	verb of fearing	μή + indicative
The subject fears that something has not happened or is not happening.	verb of fearing	μὴ οὐ + indicative

Main Verb		
The subject makes the effort that something happen.	verb of effort	ὅπως + future indicative or ὡς + future indicative
The subject makes the effort that something not happen.	verb of effort	ὅπως μή + future indicative or ὡς μή + future indicative

Translate the following sentences into Greek.

βλέπω, βλέψομαι, ἔβλεψα, βέβλεφα, βέβλεμμαι, ἐβλέφθην = to see, look | διδάσκαλος, –ου, ὁ, = teacher | πράττω (Koine πράσσω), πράξω, ἔπραξα, πέπραγμα or (πέπραχα), πέπραγμαι, ἐπράχθην = to do | τάχος, –εος, swiftness | ταχύς, –εῖα, –ύ (adj.) = swift, quick | χαλεπός, –ή, –όν (adj.) = difficult, harsh

1. Make (singular) it that you praise the courageous ones.
πρᾶττε ὅπως ἐπαινέσεις τοὺς ἀνδρείους.
πρᾶσσε ὡς ἐπαινέσεις τοὺς ἀνδρείους.

2. It being possible to hesitate, we entered.
ἐξὸν ὀκνεῖν, εἰσερχόμεθα.

3. I am afraid that the teacher will be difficult.
δέδοικα ὁ διδάσκαλος μὴ ᾖ χαλεπός.

4. I am afraid that the teacher will not be difficult.
δέδοικα ὁ διδάσκαλος μὴ οὐκ ᾖ χαλεπός.

5. See (plural) to it lest you hesitate to do courageous things.
βλέπετε ὅπως μὴ ὀκνῆτε πράττειν τὰ ἀνδρεῖα.
βλέπετε ὅπως μὴ ὀκνήσετε πράσσειν τὰ ἀνδρεῖα.

6. The teacher has swift eyes. (Use an accusative of respect.)
ὁ διδάσκαλός ἐστι ταχὺς τὰ ὄμματα.

7. I am afraid that we have not done courageous things.

δέδοικα μὴ οὐ ἐπράττομεν τὰ ἀνδρεῖα.

δέδοικα μὴ οὐ ἐπράσσομεν τὰ ἀνδρεῖα.

Chapter 39 ~

1. τὰ μὲν διδακτὰ μανθάνω, τὰ δ᾽ εὑρετὰ ζητῶ, τὰ δ᾽ εὐκτὰ παρὰ θεῶν ἠτησάμην. (Sophocles, *Fragments*)
I understand the teachable things, and I seek discoverable things, and I sought things desired from the gods.
I am learning teachable things, I am seeking things to be found, but I asked for wished things from the gods.

2. καλῶν οὐδὲν ἄνευ πόνου καὶ ἐπιμελείας οἱ θεοὶ διδόασιν ἀνθρώποις, ἀλλ᾽ εἴτε τοὺς θεοὺς ἵλεως εἶναί σοι βούλει, θεραπευτέον τοὺς θεούς, εἴτε ὑπὸ φίλων ἐθέλεις ἀγαπᾶσθαι, τοὺς φίλους εὐεργετητέον, εἴτε ὑπό τινος πόλεως ἐπιθυμεῖς τιμᾶσθαι, τὴν πόλιν ὠφελητέον. (Prodicus, in Stobaeus, *Anthology*)
The gods give nothing of beautiful things to humans without toil and care, but if you want the gods to be kind to you, you must take care of the gods. If you want to be loved by friends, you must show kindness to friends, and if you desire to be honored by some city, you must benefit the city.
The gods give nothing beautiful to men without toil and care, but if you want the gods to be kind to you, take care of the gods. If you want to be loved by friends, show kindness to friends, and if you desire to be honored by some city, benefit the city.

3. πᾶν ἀγαθὸν αἱρετόν ἐστιν. (Musonius, in Stobaeus, *Anthology*)
Every good thing is to be chosen.
Every good thing is choiceworthy.

4. μνημονευτέον δὲ ὡς τὸ μέλλον οὔτε ἡμέτερον οὔτε πάντως οὐχ ἡμέτερον, ἵνα μήτε πάντως προσμένωμεν ὡς ἐσόμενον μήτε ἀπελπίζωμεν ὡς πάντως οὐκ ἐσόμενον. (Epicurus, in Diogenes Laertius, *Lives of Eminent Philosophers*)
It must be remembered that the future is neither ours nor completely not ours, so that we neither wholly wait as though it will be, nor despair that it will wholly not be.
We must remember that the future is neither ours nor completely not ours, so that we neither completely wait as though it will happen, nor despair that it will completely not happen.

5. ἀλλὰ οἶνον νέον εἰς ἀσκοὺς καινοὺς βλητέον. (Luke 5:38)
But new wine must be put into new wine skins.
But one must put new wine into new wine skins.

6. καλὸν οὖν τὸ ἅλας ἐὰν δὲ καὶ τὸ ἅλας μωρανθῇ, ἐν τίνι ἀρτυθήσεται; οὔτε εἰς γῆν οὔτε εἰς κοπρίαν εὔθετόν ἐστιν ἔξω βάλλουσιν αὐτό. ὁ ἔχων ὦτα ἀκούειν ἀκουέτω. (Luke 14:34–35)
Salt is good, but if even salt loses its flavor, with what will it be flavored? It is suitable for neither the earth nor the trash pile. They throw it out. The one having ears to hear, let him hear.
  • There is an error in the note on page 322. It should say "with what will it be flavored," not "what will it flavor."

7. μὴ ἀγροικότερον ᾖ τὸ ἀληθὲς εἰπεῖν. (Socrates, in Plato, *Gorgias*)
Perhaps to say a true thing is rather rustic.
Perhaps to speak the truth is quite rustic.
  • Cautious assertion

8. ἀλλὰ μὴ οὐ τοῦτ᾽ ᾖ χαλεπόν, ὦ ἄνδρες, θάνατον ἐκφυγεῖν, ἀλλὰ πολὺ χαλεπώτερον πονηρίαν. (Socrates, in Plato, *Apology*)
But perhaps this is not difficult, oh men, to escape death, but much more difficult to escape evil.
Oh gentlemen, but perhaps it is not difficult to escape death, but it is much more difficult to escape wickedness.
  • Cautious denial

9. ἐγώ εἰμι ἡ ἀνάστασις καὶ ἡ ζωή ὁ πιστεύων εἰς ἐμὲ κἂν ἀποθάνη ζήσεται, καὶ πᾶς ὁ ζῶν καὶ πιστεύων εἰς ἐμὲ οὐ μὴ ἀποθάνη εἰς τὸν αἰῶνα. (John 11:25–26)

I am the resurrection and the life, the one trusting in me, even if he dies, will live, and everyone living and trusting in me will not ever die.

I am the resurrection and the life, whoever believes in me, even if he dies, shall live, and whoever lives and believes in me will never die.

- Emphatic denial

10. λέγω δέ, πνεύματι περιπατεῖτε καὶ ἐπιθυμίαν σαρκὸς οὐ μὴ τελέσητε. (Gal 5:16)

But I say, walk in the spirit and do not fulfil the desire of the flesh.

- Emphatic denial

Supplementary Exercises

Fill in the following chart.

Cautious assertion that something is or was the case.	μή + indicative
Cautious denial that something is or was the case.	μὴ οὐ + indicative
Cautious assertion that something will be the case.	μή + subjunctive
Cautious denial that something will be the case.	μὴ οὐ + subjunctive

Translate the following sentences into Greek.

ἀλήθεια, –ας, ἡ = truth | διδάσκαλος, –ου, ὁ = teacher | μαθητής, –οῦ, ὁ = student | πόνος, –ου, ὁ = toil

1. The truth must be served. (Use a verbal adjective.)

ἡ ἀλήθεια θεραπευτέα ἐστίν.

θεραπευτέον τὴν ἀλήθειαν.

2. We must remember the truth. (Use a verbal adjective.)

μνημονευτέον τὴν ἀλήθειαν.

3. Perhaps the teacher is not wise.

ὁ διδάσκαλος μὴ οὐκ ἔστι σοφός.

μὴ οὐκ ἔστι σοφὸς ὁ διδάσκαλος.

4. Perhaps the teacher will be difficult.

ὁ διδάσκαλος μὴ ᾖ χαλεπός

5. Perhaps the teacher will not help the students.

ὁ διδάσκαλος μὴ οὐκ ὠφελῇ τοὺς μαθητάς. (present subjunctive)

ὁ διδάσκαλος μὴ οὐκ ὠφελησῇ τοὺς μαθητάς. (aorist subjunctive)

6. Perhaps we are teachable.

μὴ ἡμεῖς διδακτοί ἐσμεν.

7. You (singular) will never escape toil. (Use an emphatic denial.)

οὐ μὴ ἐκφεύξεις τὸν πόνον. (future indicative)

οὐ μὴ ἐκφεύγῃς τὸν πόνον. (present subjunctive)

οὐ μὴ ἐκφύγῃς τὸν πόνον. (aorist subjunctive)

8. Don't (plural) escape. (Use an emphatic prohibition.)

οὐ μὴ ἐκφεύγητε. (present subjunctive)

οὐ μὴ ἐκφύγητε. (aorist subjunctive)

Chapter 40 ～

1. ἐπηρώτων δὲ αὐτὸν οἱ μαθηταὶ αὐτοῦ τίς αὕτη εἴη ἡ παραβολή. (Luke 8:9)
And his students were asking him what this parable was.
But his disciples asked him what this parable meant.
  - Sequence of moods

2. καί ποτέ τινος ἀκούσας ὡς μέγιστον ἀγαθὸν εἴη τὸ πάντων ἐπιτυγχάνειν ὧν τις ἐπιθυμεῖ, εἶπε, "πολὺ δὲ μεῖζον τὸ ἐπιθυμεῖν ὧν δεῖ." (Menedemus, in Diogenes Laertius, *Lives of Eminent Philosophers*)
And having once heard from someone that the greatest good is to obtain everything which one desires, he said "but it is much greater to desire what is necessary."
And once when he heard from someone that the greatest good was to obtain everything one desires, he said "but it is much greater to desire what is necessary."
  - Sequence of moods

3. εἰπόντος τινὸς ὡς ἀεὶ τοὺς φιλοσόφους βλέποι παρὰ ταῖς τῶν πλουσίων θύραις, "καὶ γὰρ οἱ ἰατροί," φησί, "παρὰ ταῖς τῶν νοσούντων· ἀλλ' οὐ παρὰ τοῦτό τις ἂν ἕλοιτο νοσεῖν ἢ ἰατρεύειν." (Aristippus, in Diogenes Laertius, *Lives of Eminent Philosophers*)
Someone having once said that he always saw philosophers at the doors of the rich, he (Aristippus) said "and physicians at the doors of the sick, but not for this reason would one choose to be sick rather than a doctor."

When someone once said that he always sees philosophers at the doors of the rich, he (Aristippus) said "and we see physicians at the doors of the sick, but not for this reason would we choose to be sick rather than a doctor."

- Sequence of moods in the first clause
- Potential optative in the last clause

4. ὁμοίως καὶ πρὸς τὸν εἰπόντα ὅτι κίνησις οὐκ ἔστιν, ἀναστὰς περιεπάτει. (Diogenes Laertius, *Lives of Eminent Philosophers*)

And likewise, to one saying that motion does not exist, having gotten up, he was walking around.

And likewise, in response to someone who said there is not motion, he got up and started walking around.

- Sequence of moods not used by the author

5. ὁ δὲ εἶπεν, "Λέγω σοι, Πέτρε, οὐ φωνήσει σήμερον ἀλέκτωρ ἕως τρίς με ἀπαρνήσῃ εἰδέναι." (Luke 22:34)

And he said, "I say to you, Peter, the cock will not make a sound until you deny to know me three times."

And he said, "I say to you, Peter, the cock will not crow until you deny me three times."

- Temporal clause with the subjunctive because the action has not yet happened at the time of the statement.

6. αὐτός, ὦ Φαίδων, παρεγένου Σωκράτει ἐκείνῃ τῇ ἡμέρᾳ ᾗ τὸ φάρμακον ἔπιεν ἐν τῷ δεσμωτηρίῳ; (Plato, *Phaedo*)

Were you yourself, Phaedrus, with Socrates on that day on which he drank poison in the prison?

- Temporal clause with the indicative because the action has happened at the time of the statement.

7. Χαιρεφῶν ποτε καὶ εἰς Δελφοὺς ἐλθὼν ἐτόλμησε τοῦτο μαντεύσασθαι—καί, ὅπερ λέγω, μὴ θορυβεῖτε, ὦ ἄνδρες—ἤρετο γὰρ δὴ εἴ τις ἐμοῦ εἴη σοφώτερος. ἀνεῖλεν οὖν ἡ Πυθία μηδένα σοφώτερον εἶναι. (Socrates, in Plato, *Apology*)

Once Chaerophon, going to Delphi dared to ask the Oracle this—and gentlemen, don't make an uproar at what I say—for he asked then if anyone were wiser than me. Then the Pythia replied that no one was wiser.

Once Chaerophon went to Delphi and dared to ask the Oracle this - and gentlemen, don't make an uproar at what I say- for he then asked if anyone is wiser than me. Then the Pythia replied that no one is wiser.

- Sequence of moods

8.   γὰρ ἐὰν ἐσθίητε τὸν ἄρτον τοῦτον καὶ τὸ ποτήριον πίνητε, τὸν θάνατον τοῦ κυρίου καταγγέλλετε, ἄχρις οὗ ἔλθῃ. (1 Cor 11:26)

For as often as you eat this bread and drink this cup, you proclaim the death of the Lord, until the time in which he comes.

For whenever you eat this bread and drink this cup, you proclaim the death of the Lord, until he comes again.

- Temporal clause with the subjunctive because the action has not yet happened at the time of the statement.

9.   μήπω μέγαν εἴπῃς πρὶν τελευτήσαντ᾿ ἴδῃς. (Sophocles, in Stobaeus, *Anthology*)

Do not call one great until you see that he has died.

Don't call a man great until you see him dead.

- εἴπῃς is a prohibitive subjunctive, and ἴδῃς is a temporal clause with the subjunctive because the action has not yet happened at the time of the statement.

10. οὐ μὲν γάρ ποτ᾿ ἔφασκε γῆς καρπὸν ἀνήσειν, πρὶν ἴδοι ὀφθαλμοῖσιν ἐὴν εὐώπιδα κούρην. (*Homeric Hymn to Demeter*)

For she denied that she would ever send up the fruit of the earth until she saw her fair-eyed daughter with her own eyes.

- There are two ways to explain the optative, which are not mutually exclusive.
    1—Temporal clause with the optative because the action has not yet happened at the time of the statement and the action is viewed as not likely.

2—Temporal clause with the subjunctive because the action has not yet happened at the time of the statement, which is switched to the optative because of sequence of moods.

Supplementary Exercises

In accordance with sequence of moods, change the verbs in secondary sequence into the optative.

1. ἐφιλοσόφουν ἵνα γένωμαι εὐδαίμων.
ἐφιλοσόφουν ἵνα γενοίμην εὐδαίμων.

2. οἱ φιλόσοφοι ἔλεγον ὅτι Σωκράτης βλάψει τοὺς μαθητάς.
οἱ φιλόσοφοι ἔλεγον ὅτι Σωκράτης βλάψοι τοὺς μαθητάς.

3. εἴπομεν ποῦ ἐστε.
εἴπομεν ποῦ εἶτε.
εἴπομεν ποῦ εἴητε.

4. εἶδον τί πράττεις.
εἶδον τί πράττοις.

Translate the following sentences into Greek.
ἀποθνῄσκω, ἀποθανοῦμαι, ἀπέθανον, τέθνηκα = to die | ὁράω (imperf. ἑώρων), ὄψομαι, εἶδον = to see | Σωκράτης, –ους, ὁ = Socrates | εὖ (adv.) = well | φιλοσοφέω, φιλοσοφήσω, ἐφιλοσόφησα, πεφιλοσόφηκα, πεφιλοσόφημαι, ἐφιλοσοφήθην = to philosophize

1. I said that we desired the cup.
εἶπον ὅτι ἐπεθυμοῦμεν τὸ ποτήριον.
εἶπον ὅτι ἐπιθυμοῖμεν τὸ ποτήριον. (sequence of moods)

2. Socrates philosophized in order to die well.
ὁ Σωκράτης ἐφιλοσόφει ἵνα εὖ ἀποθάνῃ.
ὁ Σωκράτης ἐφιλοσόφει ἵνα εὖ ἀποθάνοι. (sequence of moods)

3. I saw where you met Socrates.

εἶδον ὅπου ἐπέτυχες τῷ Σωκράτει.

εἶδον ὅπου ἐπιτύχοις τῷ Σωκράτει. (sequence of moods)

4. We will philosophize until we die.

φιλοσοφήσομεν πρὶν ἀποθάνωμεν ἄν.

5. He philosophized until he died.

ἐφιλοσόφει πρὶν ἀπέθανεν.

6. He philosophized before he died.

ἐφιλοσόφει πρὶν ἀποθανεῖν.

Conjugation of λύω

The Indicative

	Present Active Indicative	Future Active Indicative	Imperfect Active Indicative	Aorist Active Indicative
Singular	Singular	Singular	Singular	Singular
1st pers.	λύω	λύσω	ἔλυον	ἔλυσα
2nd pers.	λύεις	λύσεις	ἔλυες	ἔλυσας
3rd pers.	λύει	λύσει	ἔλυε(ν)	ἔλυσε(ν)
Plural	Plural	Plural	Plural	Plural
1st pers.	λύομεν	λύσομεν	ἐλύομεν	ἐλύσαμεν
2nd pers.	λύετε	λύσετε	ἐλύετε	ἐλύσατε
3rd pers.	λύουσι(ν)	λύσουσι(ν)	ἔλυον	ἔλυσαν

	Present Middle Indicative	Future Middle Indicative	Imperfect Middle Indicative	Aorist Middle Indicative
Singular	Singular	Singular	Singular	Singular
1st pers.	λύομαι	λύσομαι	ἐλυόμην	ἐλυσάμην
2nd pers.	λύῃ/ει	λύσῃ/ει	ἐλύου	ἐλύσω
3rd pers.	λύεται	λύσεται	ἐλύετο	ἐλύσατο
Plural	Plural	Plural	Plural	Singular
1st pers.	λυόμεθα	λυσόμεθα	ἐλυόμεθα	ἐλυσάμεθα
2nd pers.	λύεσθε	λύσεσθε	ἐλύεσθε	ἐλύσασθε
3rd pers.	λύονται	λύσονται	ἐλύοντο	ἐλύσαντο

	Present Passive Indicative	Future Passive Indicative	Imperfect Passive Indicative	Aorist Passive Indicative
Singular	Singular	Singular	Singular	Singular
1st pers.	λύομαι	λυθήσομαι	ἐλυόμην	ἐλύθην
2nd pers.	λύῃ/ει	λυθήσῃ/σει	ἐλύου	ἐλύθης
3rd pers.	λύεται	λυθήσεται	ἐλύετο	ἐλύθη
Plural	Plural	Plural	Plural	Plural
1st pers.	λυόμεθα	λυθησόμεθα	ἐλυόμεθα	ἐλύθημεν
2nd pers.	λύεσθε	λυθήσεσθε	ἐλύεσθε	ἐλύθητε
3rd pers.	λύονται	λυθήσονται	ἐλύοντο	ἐλύθησαν

	Perfect Active Indicative	Pluperfect Active Indicative	Future Perfect Active Indicative
Singular	Singular	Singular	Singular
1st pers.	λέλυκα	ἐλελύκη	λελυκὼς[1] ἔσομαι
2nd pers.	λέλυκας	ἐλελύκης	λελυκὼς ἔσῃ (ἔσει)
3rd pers.	λέλυκε(ν)	ἐλελύκει(ν)	λελυκὼς ἔσται
Plural	Plural	Plural	Plural
1st pers.	λελύκαμεν	ἐλελύκεμεν	λελυκότες ἐσόμεθα
2nd pers.	λελύκατε	ἐλελύκετε	λελυκότες ἔσεσθε
3rd pers.	λελύκασι(ν)	ἐλελύκεσαν	λελυκότες ἔσονται

	Perfect Middle Indicative	Pluperfect Middle Indicative	Future Perfect Middle Indicative
Singular	Singular	Singular	Singular
1st pers.	λέλυμαι	ἐλελύμην	λελυμένος ἔσομαι
2nd pers.	λέλυσαι	ἐλέλυσο	λελυμένος ἔσῃ (ἔσει)
3rd pers.	λέλυται	ἐλέλυτο	λελυμένος ἔσται
Plural	Plural	Plural	Plural
1st pers.	λελύμεθα	ἐλελύμεθα	λελυμένοι ἐσόμεθα
2nd pers.	λέλυσθε	ἐλέλυσθε	λελυμένοι ἔσεσθε
3rd pers.	λέλυνται	ἐλέλυντο	λελυμένοι ἔσονται

	Perfect Passive Indicative	Pluperfect Passive Indicative	Future Perfect Passive Indicative
Singular	Singular	Singular	Singular
1st pers.	λέλυμαι	ἐλελύμην	λελύσομαι
2nd pers.	λέλυσαι	ἐλέλυσο	λελύσῃ/ λελύσει
3rd pers.	λέλυται	ἐλέλυτο	λελύσεται
Plural	Plural	Plural	Plural
1st pers.	λελύμεθα	ἐλελύμεθα	λελυσόμεθα
2nd pers.	λέλυσθε	ἐλέλυσθε	λελύσεσθε
3rd pers.	λέλυνται	ἐλέλυντο	λελύσονται

---

[1] The gender of the participle must match the gender of the subject.

The Subjunctive

	Present Active Subjunctive	Present Middle/Passive Subjunctive	Perfect Active Subjunctive	Perfect Middle/Passive Subjunctive
Singular	Singular	Singular	Singular	Singular
1st pers.	λύω	λύωμαι	λελύκω[2]	λελυμένος ὦ
2nd pers.	λύῃς	λύῃ	λελύκῃς	λελυμένος ᾖς
3rd pers.	λύῃ	λύηται	λελύκη	λελυμένος ᾖ
Plural	Plural	Plural	Plural	Plural
1st pers.	λύωμεν	λυώμεθα	λελύκωμεν	λελυμένοι ὦμεν
2nd pers.	λύητε	λύησθε	λελύκητε	λελυμένοι ἦτε
3rd pers.	λύωσι(ν)	λύωνται	λελύκωσι(ν)	λελυμένοι ὦσι(ν)

	Aorist Active Subjunctive	Aorist Middle Subjunctive	Aorist Passive Subjunctive
Singular	Singular	Singular	Singular
1st pers.	λύσω	λύσωμαι	λυθῶ
2nd pers.	λύσῃς	λύσῃ	λυθῇς
3rd pers.	λύσῃ	λύσηται	λυθῇ
Plural	Plural	Plural	Plural
1st pers.	λύσωμεν	λυσώμεθα	λυθῶμεν
2nd pers.	λύσητε	λύσησθε	λυθῆτε
3rd pers.	λύσωσι(ν)	λύσωνται	λυθῶσι (ν)

---

[2] All the perfect subjunctives can be formed periphrastically with the perfect participle + the subjunctive of εἰμί, i.e. λελυκὼς ὦ, λελυκὼς ᾖς, λελυκὼς ᾖ, etc.

The Optative

	Present Active Optative	Present Middle/Passive Optative	Perfect Active Optative	Perfect Middle/Passive Optative
Singular	Singular	Singular	Singular	Singular
1ˢᵗ pers.	λύοιμι	λυοίμην	λελύκοιμι[3]	λελυμένος εἴην
2ⁿᵈ pers.	λύοις	λύοιο	λελύκοις	λελυμένος εἴης
3ʳᵈ pers.	λύοι	λύοιτο	λελύκοι	λελυμένος εἴη
Plural	Plural	Plural	Plural	Plural
1ˢᵗ pers.	λύοιμεν	λυοίμεθα	λελύκοιμεν	λελυμένοι εἶμεν/ εἴημεν
2ⁿᵈ pers.	λύοιτε	λύοισθε	λελύκοιτε	λελυμένοι εἶτε/ εἴητε
3ʳᵈ pers.	λύοιεν	λύοιντο	λελύκοιεν	λελυμένοι εἶεν/ εἴησαν

	Future Active Optative	Future Middle Optative	Future Passive Optative
Singular	Singular	Singular	Singular
1ˢᵗ pers.	λύσοιμι	λυσοίμην	λυθησοίμην
2ⁿᵈ pers.	λύσοις	λύσοιο	λυθήσοιο
3ʳᵈ pers.	λύσοι	λύσοιτο	λυθήσοιτο
Plural	Plural	Plural	Plural
1ˢᵗ pers.	λύσοιμεν	λυσοίμεθα	λυθησοίμεθα
2ⁿᵈ pers.	λύσοιτε	λύσοισθε	λυθήσοισθε
3ʳᵈ pers.	λύσοιεν	λύσοιντο	λυθήσοιντο

	Aorist Active Optative	Aorist Middle Optative	Aorist Passive Optative
Singular	Singular	Singular	Singular
1ˢᵗ pers.	λύσαιμι	λυσαίμην	λυθείην
2ⁿᵈ pers.	λύσειας (λύσαις)	λύσαιο	λυθείης
3ʳᵈ pers.	λύσειε(ν) (λύσαι)	λύσαιτο	λυθείη
Plural	Plural	Plural	Plural
1ˢᵗ pers.	λύσαιμεν	λυσαίμεθα	λυθείημεν (λυθεῖμεν)
2ⁿᵈ pers.	λύσαιτε	λύσαισθε	λυθείητε (λυθεῖτε)
3ʳᵈ pers.	λύσειαν (λύσαιεν)	λύσαιντο	λυθείησαν (λυθεῖεν)

---

[3] All the perfect optatives can be formed periphrastically with the perfect participle + the optative of εἰμί, i.e. λελυκὼς εἴην, λελυκὼς εἴης, λελυκὼς εἴη, etc.

The Imperative

	Present Active Imperative	Present Middle/Passive Imperative
Singular	Singular	Singular
2nd pers.	λῦε	λύου
3rd pers.	λυέτω	λυέσθω
Plural	Plural	Plural
2nd pers.	λύετε	λύεσθε
3rd pers.	λυόντων	λυέσθων

	Aorist Active Imperative	Aorist Middle Imperative	Aorist Passive Imperative
Singular	Singular	Singular	Singular
2nd pers.	λῦσον	λῦσαι	λύθητι
3rd pers.	λυσάτω	λυσάσθω	λυθήτω
Plural	Plural	Plural	Plural
2nd pers.	λύσατε	λύσασθε	λύθητε
3rd pers.	λυσάντων	λυσάσθων	λυθέντων

	Perfect Active Imperative	Perfect Middle/Passive Imperative
Singular	Singular	Singular
2nd pers.	λέλυκε	λέλυσο
3rd pers.	λελυκέτω	λελύσθω
Plural	Plural	Plural
2nd pers.	λελύκετε	λελύσθε
3rd pers.	λελυκότες ὄντων[4]	λελύσθων

---

[4] All the perfect imperatives can be formed periphrastically like the 3rd person plural.

The Infinitive

Present Active Infinitive	Present Middle Infinitive
λύειν	λύεσθαι

Future Active Infinitive	Future Middle Infinitive	Future Passive Infinitive
λύσειν	λύσεσθαι	λυθήσεσθαι

Aorist Active Infinitive	Aorist Middle Infinitive	Aorist Passive Infinitive
λῦσαι	λύσασθαι	λυθῆναι

Perfect Active Infinitive	Perfect Middle Infinitive	Perfect Passive Infinitive
λελυκέναι	λελύσθαι	λελύσθαι

Future Perfect Passive Infinitive
λελύσεσθαι